SUPER
EASY
SONGBOOK

THE BEATLES

ISBN 978-1-4950-7623-7

HAL•LEONARD®

7777 W. BLUEMOUND RD. P.O. BOX 13819 MILWAUKEE, WI 53213

In Australia Contact:
Hal Leonard Australia Pty. Ltd.
4 Lentara Court
Cheltenham, Victoria, 3192 Australia
Email: ausadmin@halleonard.com.au

Visit Hal Leonard Online at
www.halleonard.com

Welcome to the *Super Easy Songbook* series!

This unique collection will help you play your favorite songs quickly and easily. Here's how it works:

- Play the simplified melody with your right hand. Letter names appear inside each note to assist you.

- There are no key signatures to worry about! If a sharp ♯ or flat ♭ is needed, it is shown beside the note each time.

- There are no page turns, so your hands never have to leave the keyboard.

- If two notes are connected by a tie ⌣, hold the first note for the combined number of beats. (The second note does not show a letter name since it is not re-struck.)

- Add basic chords with your left hand using the provided keyboard diagrams. Chord voicings have been carefully chosen to minimize hand movement.

- The left-hand rhythm is up to you, and chord notes can be played together or separately. Be creative!

- If the chords sound muddy, move your left hand an octave* higher. If this gets in the way of playing the melody, move your right hand an octave higher as well.

    * *An octave spans eight notes. If your starting note is C, the next C to the right is an octave higher.*

―――――――――――――――― ALSO AVAILABLE ――――――――――――――――

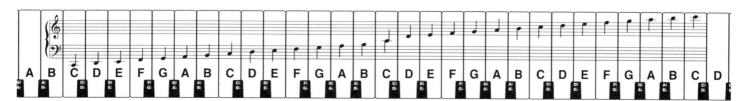

Hal Leonard Student Keyboard Guide HL00296039

Key Stickers HL00100016

Across the Universe

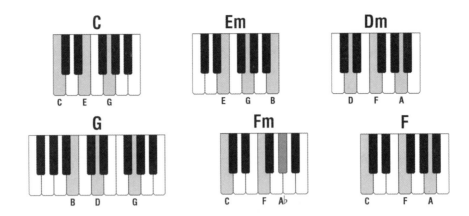

Words and Music by John Lennon
and Paul McCartney

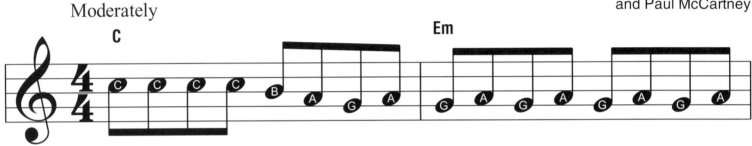

Words are flow - ing out like end - less rain in - to a pa - per cup. They

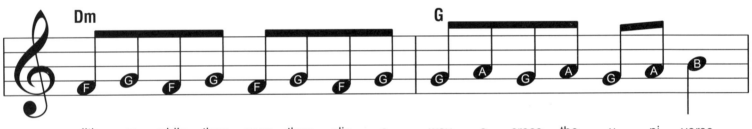

slith - er while they pass, they slip a - way a - cross the u - ni - verse.

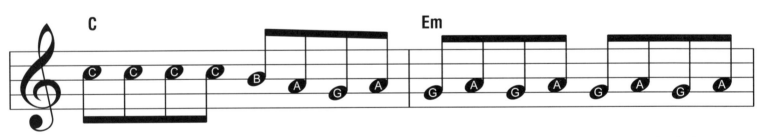

Pools of sor - row, waves of joy are drift - ing through my o - pened mind, pos -

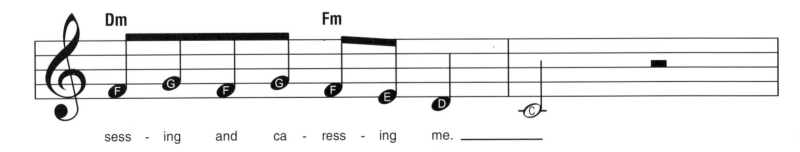

sess - ing and ca - ress - ing me. _____

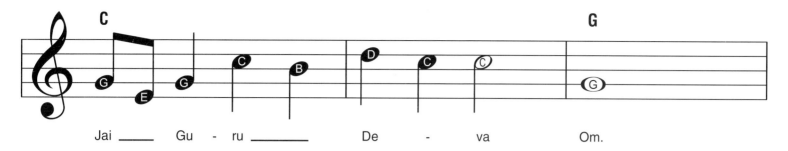

Jai _____ Gu - ru _____ De - va Om.

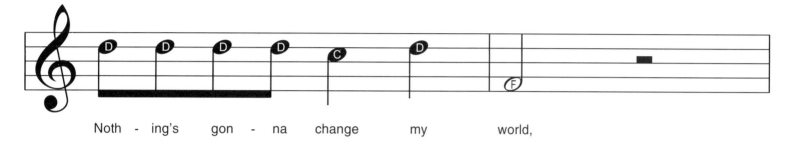

Noth - ing's gon - na change my world,

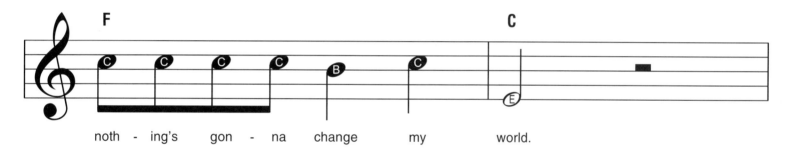

noth - ing's gon - na change my world.

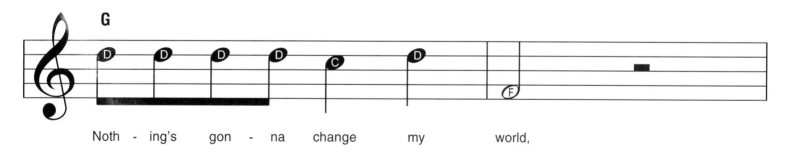

Noth - ing's gon - na change my world,

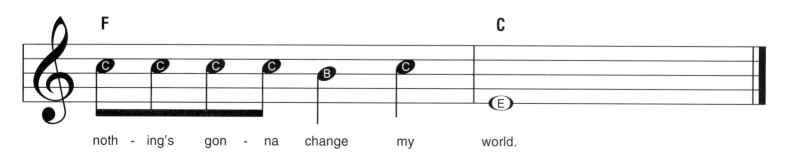

noth - ing's gon - na change my world.

All My Loving

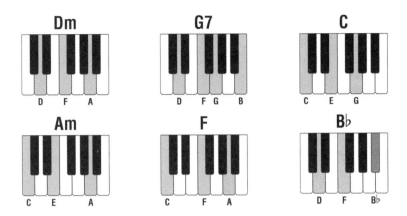

Words and Music by John Lennon
and Paul McCartney

Moderately

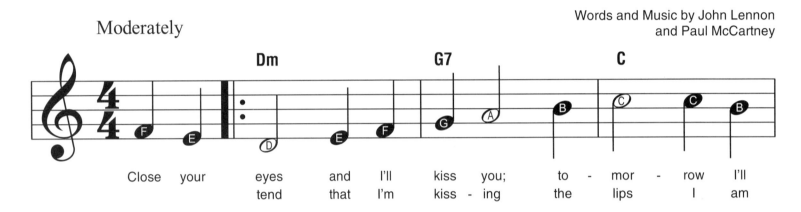

Close your eyes and I'll kiss you; to - mor - row I'll
tend that I'm kiss - ing to the lips I am

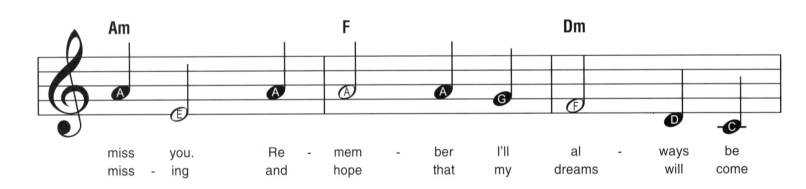

miss you. Re - mem - ber I'll al - ways be
miss - ing and hope that my dreams will come

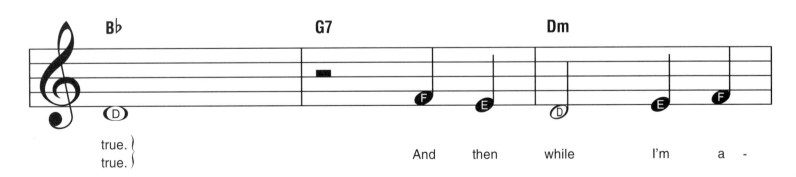

true.
true. }

And then while I'm a -

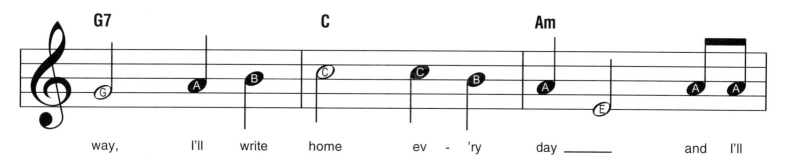

way, I'll write home ev - 'ry day _____ and I'll

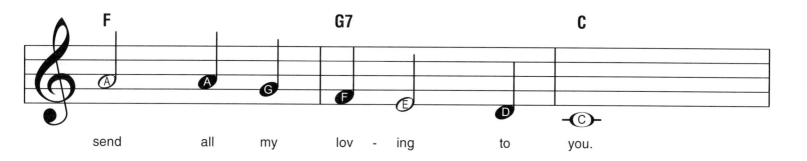

send all my lov - ing to you.

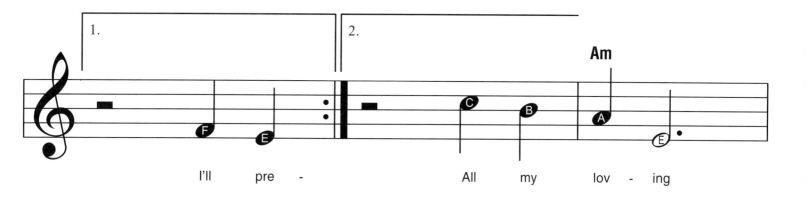

I'll pre -   All my lov - ing

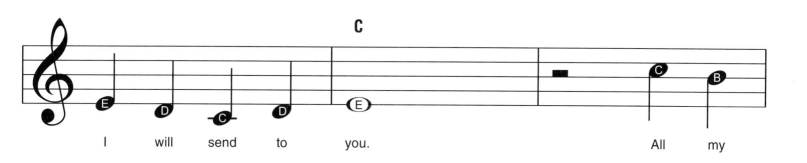

I will send to you.   All my

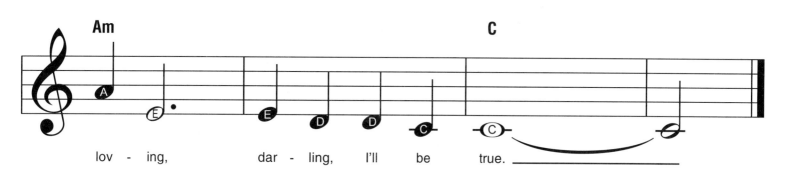

lov - ing, dar - ling, I'll be true. _____

All You Need Is Love

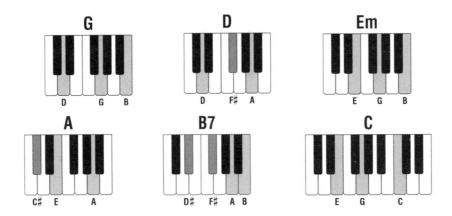

Words and Music by John Lennon
and Paul McCartney

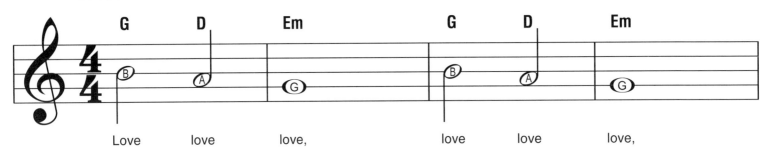

Love   love   love,   love   love   love,

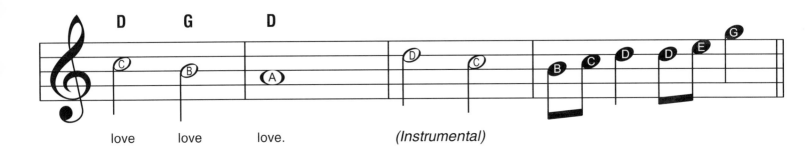

love   love   love.   (Instrumental)

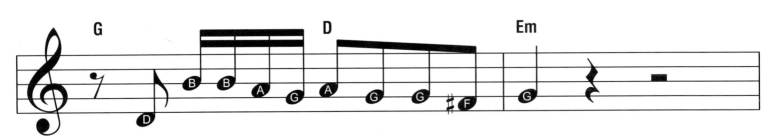

There's noth-ing you can do that can't be done,

nothing you can sing that can't be sung.

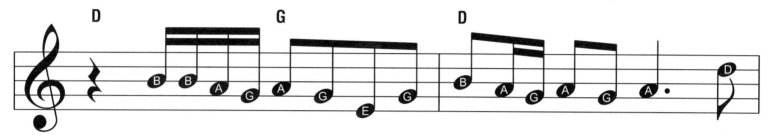

Noth-ing you can say, but you can learn how to play the game. It's

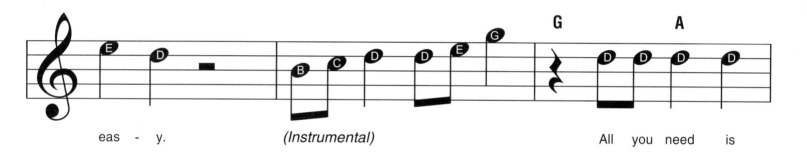

eas - y.   *(Instrumental)*   All you need is

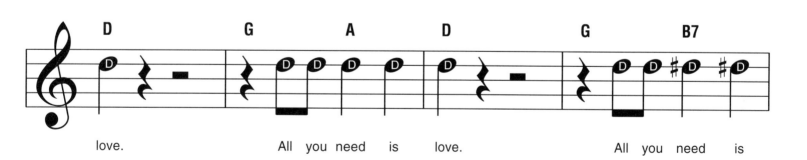

love.   All you need is love.   All you need is

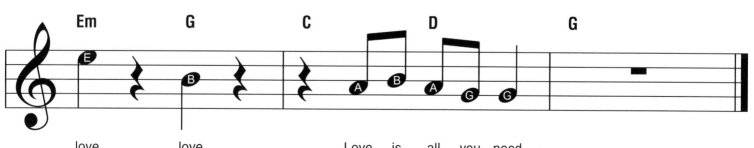

love,   love.   Love is all you need.

And I Love Her

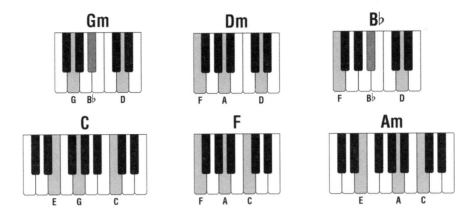

Words and Music by John Lennon
and Paul McCartney

Moderately

I give her all my love, that's all I
She gives me ev - 'ry - thing, and ten - der -

do. _____
ly. _____

And if you saw my love,
The kiss my lov - er brings,

you'd love her too, _____ and I love her.
she brings to me, _____ and I love her.

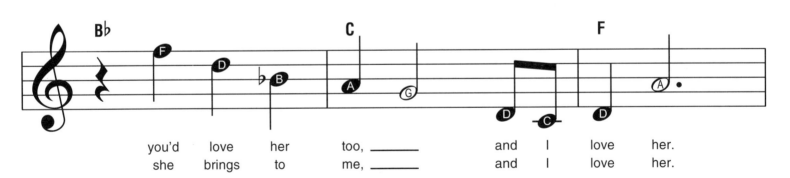

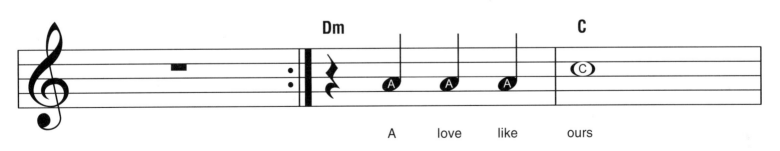

A love like ours

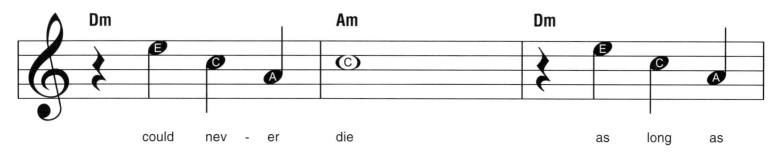

could nev - er die   as long as

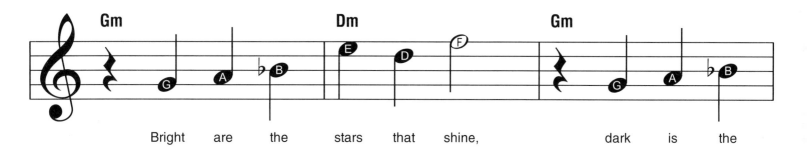

I   have   you   near   me.

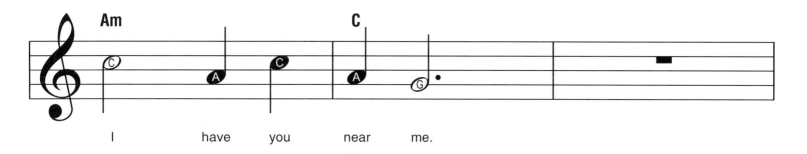

Bright   are   the   stars   that   shine,   dark   is   the

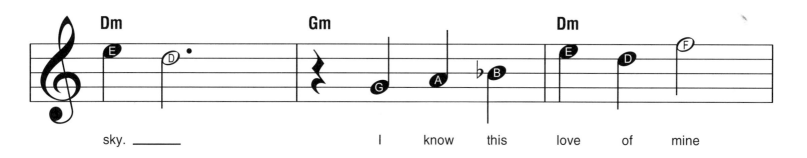

sky. ____   I   know   this   love   of   mine

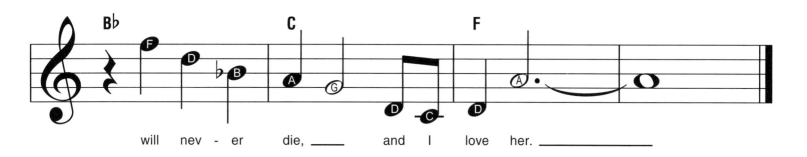

will   nev - er   die, ____   and   I   love   her. _____

Back in the U.S.S.R.

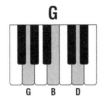
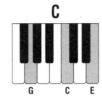
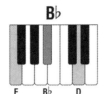
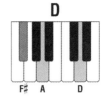

Words and Music by John Lennon
and Paul McCartney

Moderate Rock

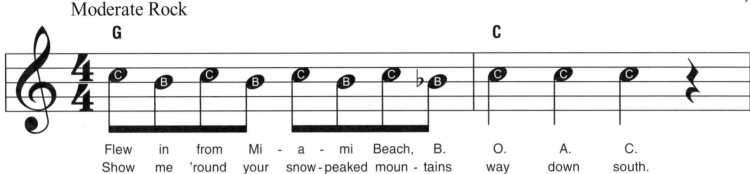

Flew in from Mi - a - mi Beach, B. O. A. C.
Show me 'round your snow - peaked moun - tains way down south.

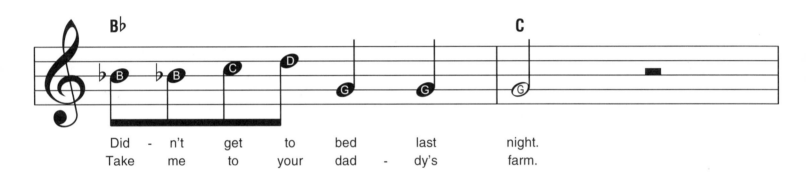

Did - n't get to bed last night.
Take me to your dad - dy's farm.

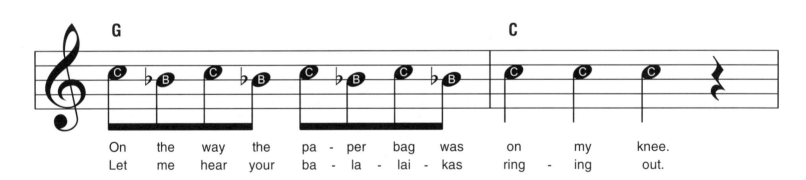

On the way the pa - per bag was on my knee.
Let me hear your ba - la - lai - kas ring - ing out.

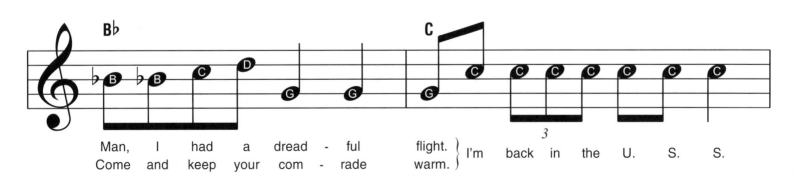

Man, I had a dread - ful flight. } I'm back in the U. S. S.
Come and keep your com - rade warm.

Blackbird

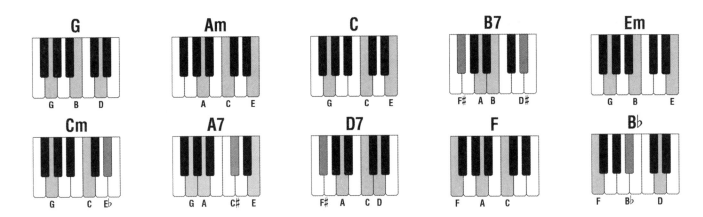

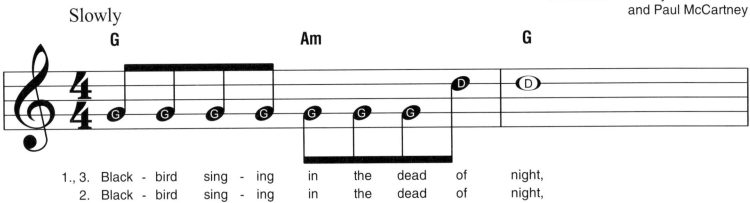

Words and Music by John Lennon
and Paul McCartney

Slowly

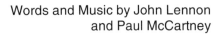

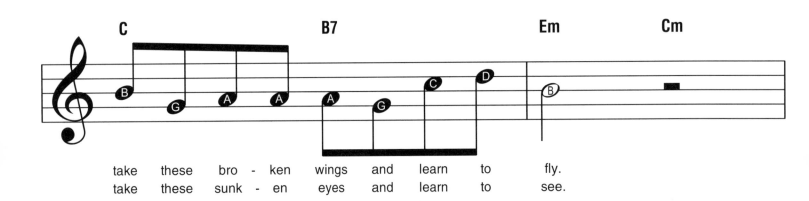

1., 3. Black - bird sing - ing in the dead of night,
2. Black - bird sing - ing in the dead of night,

take these bro - ken wings and learn to fly.
take these sunk - en eyes and learn to see.

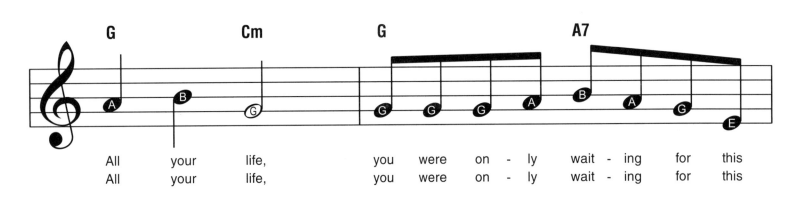

All your life, you were on - ly wait - ing for this
All your life, you were on - ly wait - ing for this

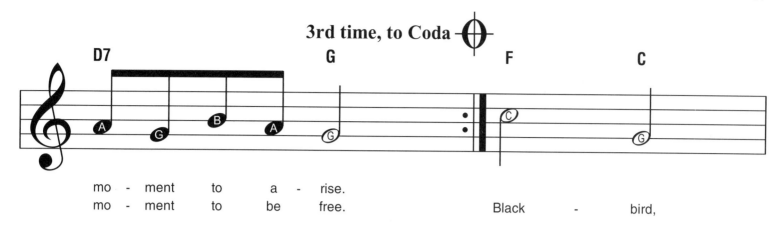

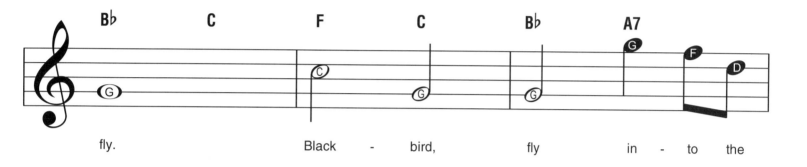

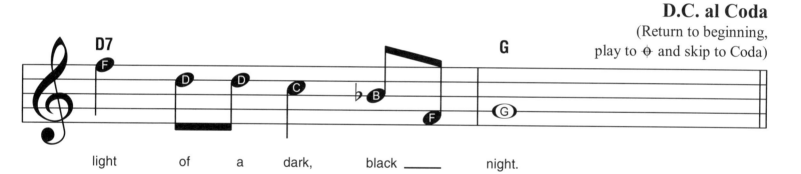

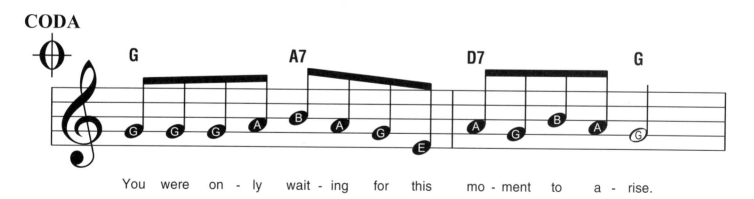

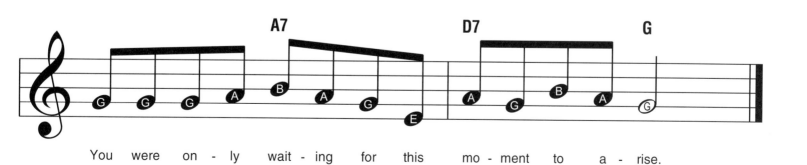

Can't Buy Me Love

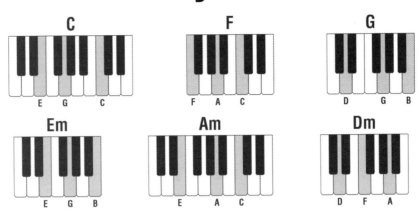

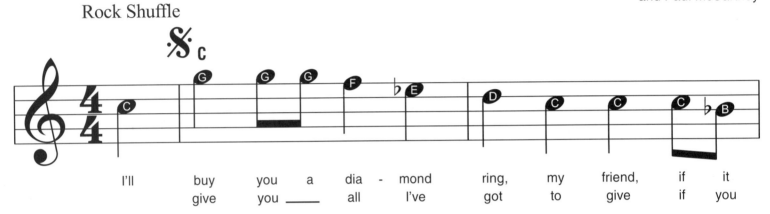

Words and Music by John Lennon
and Paul McCartney

Rock Shuffle

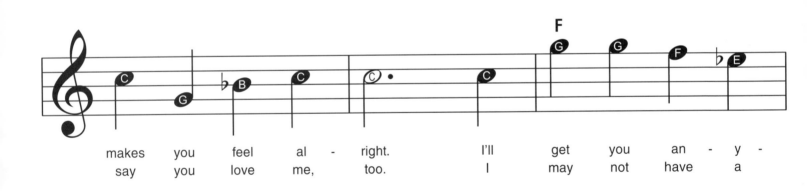

I'll buy you a dia - mond ring, my friend, if it
give you ___ all I've got to give if you

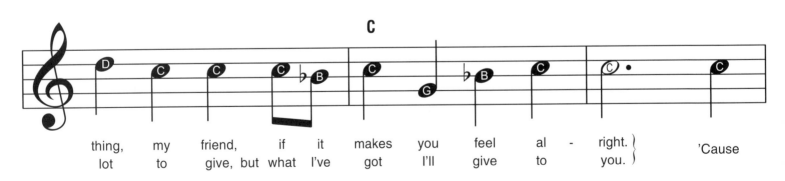

makes you feel al - right. I'll get you an - y -
say you love me, too. I may not have a

thing, my friend, if it makes you feel al - right. } 'Cause
lot to give, but what I've got I'll give al to you.

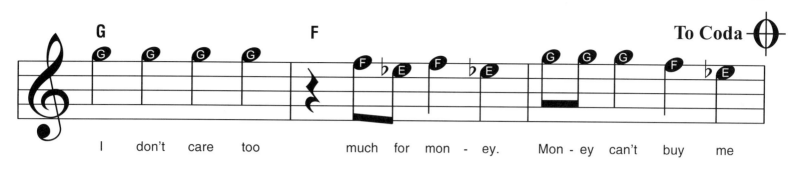

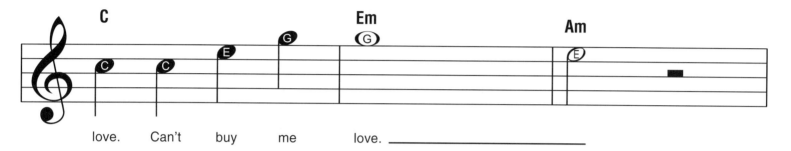

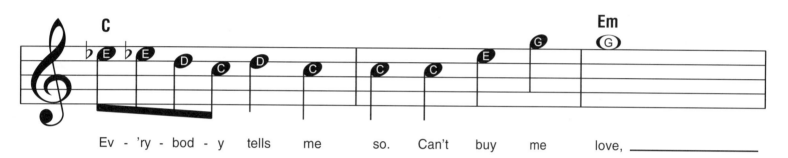

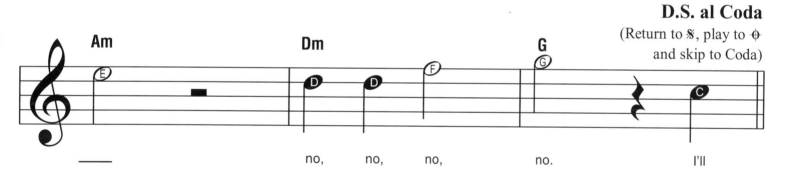

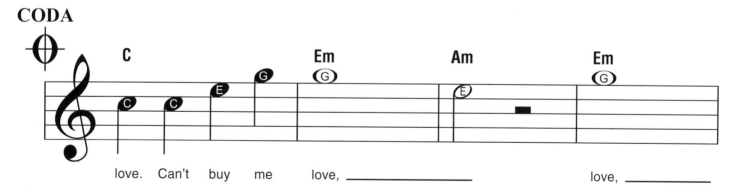

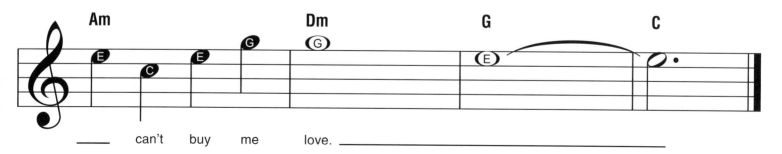

Carry That Weight

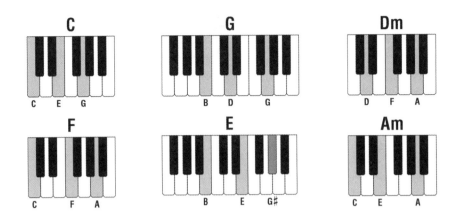

Words and Music by John Lennon
and Paul McCartney

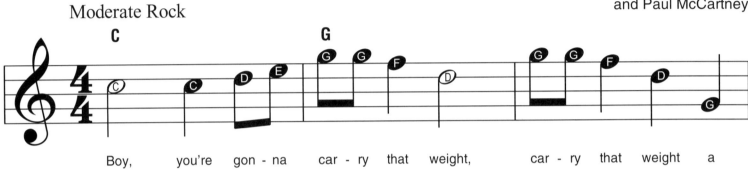

Boy, you're gon - na car - ry that weight, car - ry that weight a

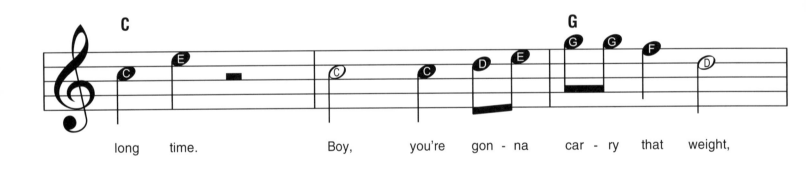

long time. Boy, you're gon - na car - ry that weight,

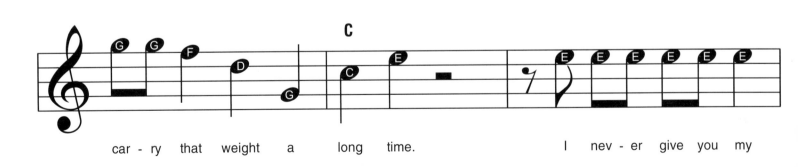

car - ry that weight a long time. I nev - er give you my

Come Together

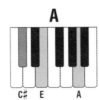
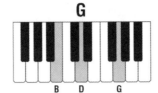
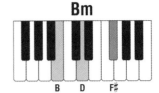

Words and Music by John Lennon
and Paul McCartney

Moderate Rock

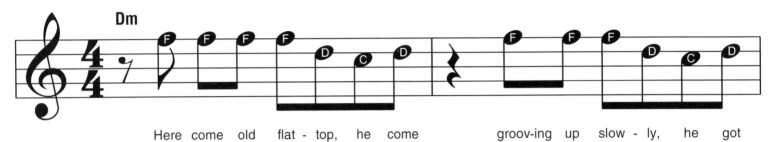

Here come old flat - top, he come groov-ing up slow - ly, he got

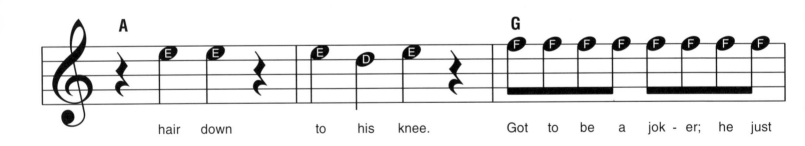

Joo Joo eye - ball, he one ho - ly roll - er. He got

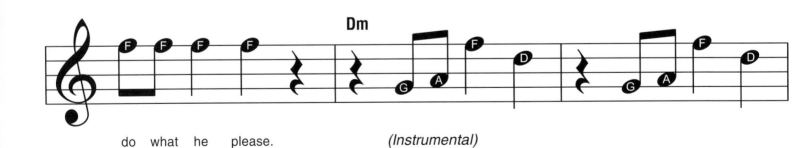

hair down to his knee. Got to be a jok - er; he just

do what he please. *(Instrumental)*

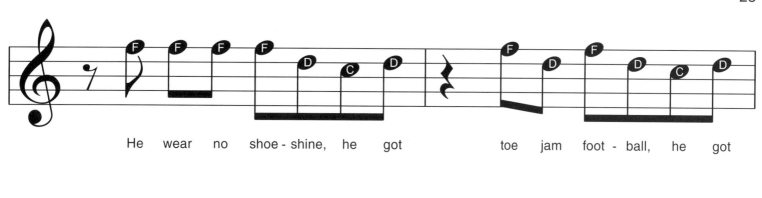

He wear no shoe - shine, he got   toe jam foot - ball, he got

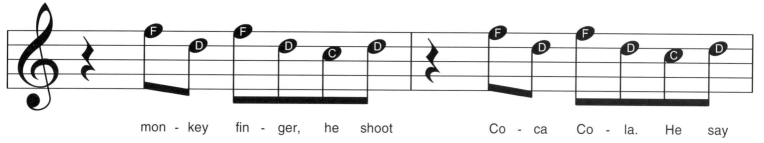

mon - key fin - ger, he shoot   Co - ca Co - la.   He say

I   know ____ you,   you   know ____ me.

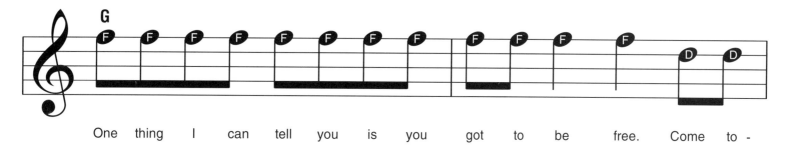

One   thing   I   can   tell   you   is   you   got   to   be   free.   Come   to -

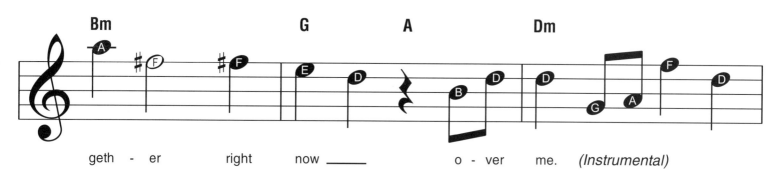

geth - er   right   now ____   o - ver   me.   *(Instrumental)*

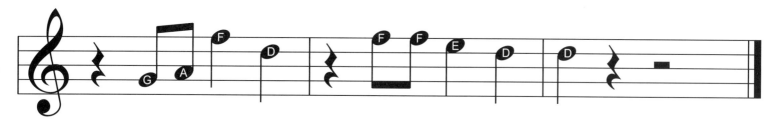

Come   to - geth - er,   yeah!

Day Tripper

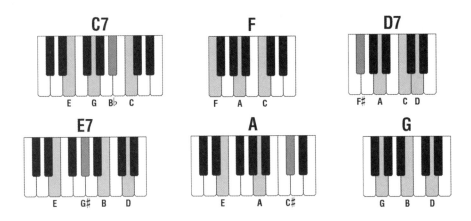

Words and Music by John Lennon
and Paul McCartney

Moderate Rock

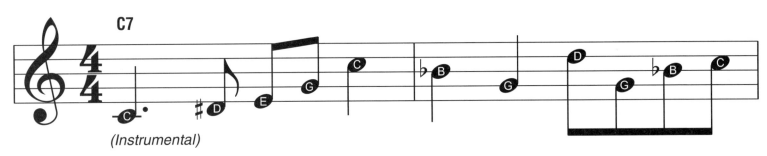

(Instrumental)

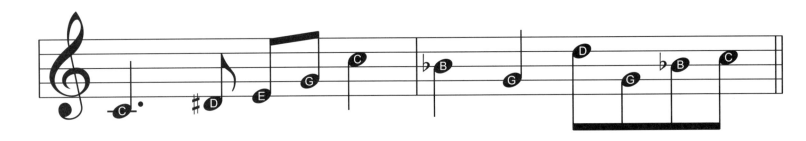

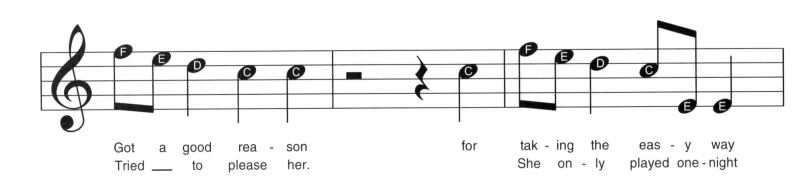

Got a good rea - son ___ for tak - ing the eas - y way
Tried ___ to please her. ___ She on - ly played one - night

Do You Want to Know a Secret?

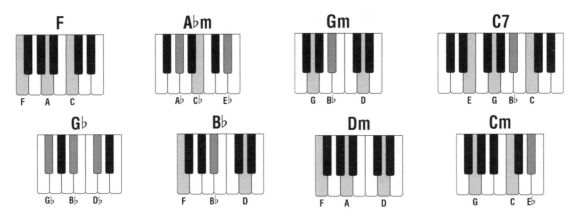

Words and Music by John Lennon
and Paul McCartney

Moderately

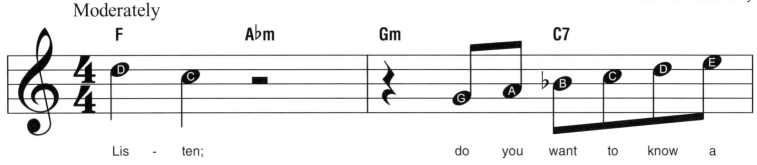

Lis - ten; do you want to know a

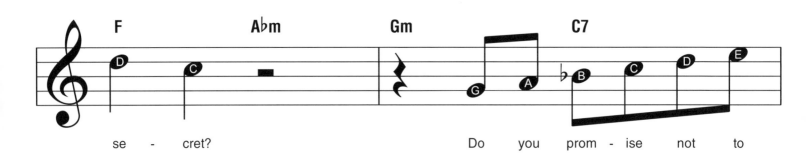

se - cret? Do you prom - ise not to

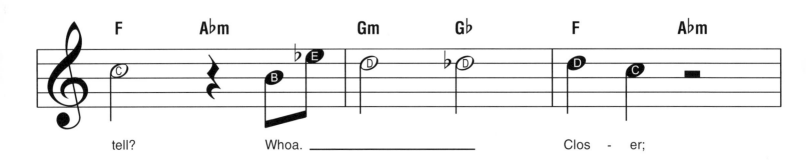

tell? Whoa. _____ Clos - er;

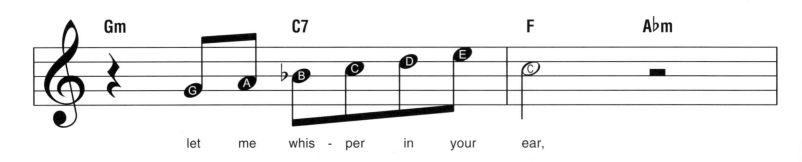

let me whis - per in your ear,

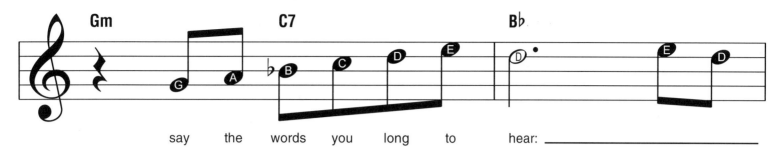

say the words you long to hear: _____

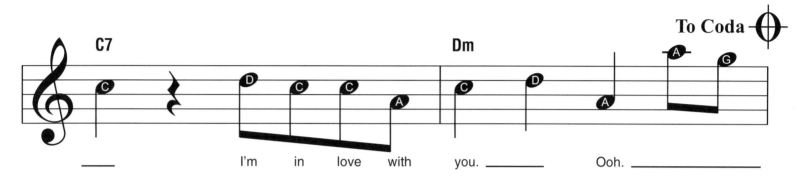

To Coda ⊕

____ I'm in love with you. _____ Ooh. _____

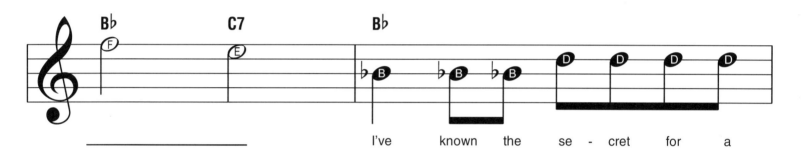

_____ I've known the se - cret for a

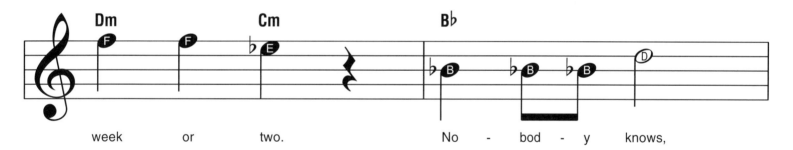

week or two. No - bod - y knows,

D.C. al Coda
(Return to beginning,
play to ⊕ and skip to Coda)

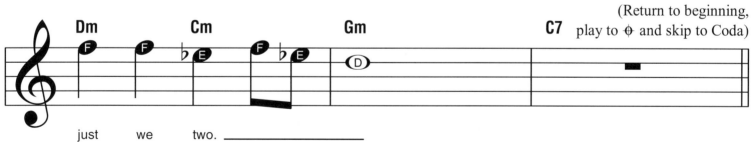

just we two. _____

CODA ⊕

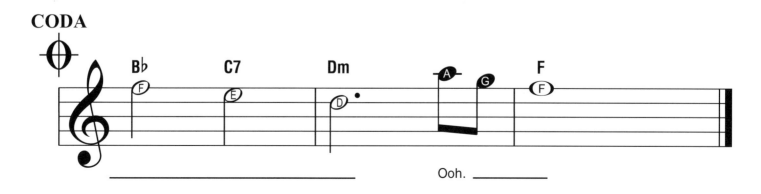

Ooh. _____

Eight Days a Week

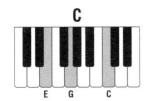 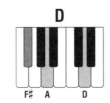 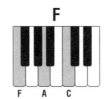 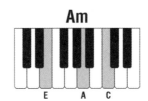 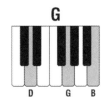

Words and Music by John Lennon
and Paul McCartney

Moderately bright

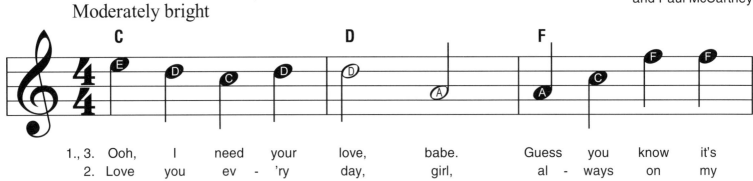

1., 3. Ooh, I need your love, babe. Guess you know it's
2. Love you ev - 'ry day, girl, al - ways on my

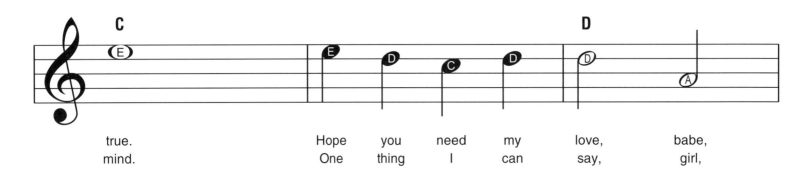

true. Hope you need my love, babe,
mind. One thing I can say, girl,

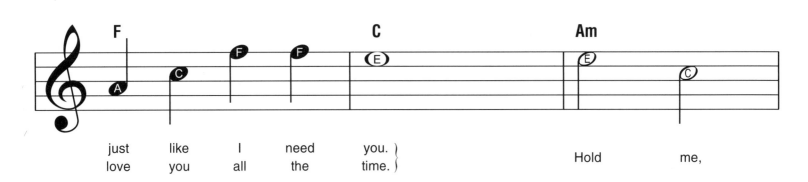

just like I need you.)
love you all the time.)

Hold me,

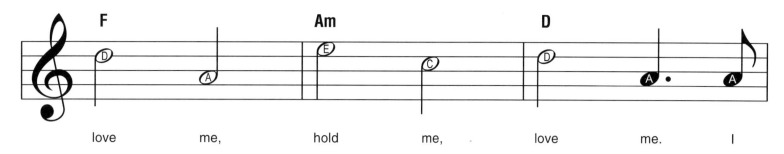

love me, hold me, love me. I

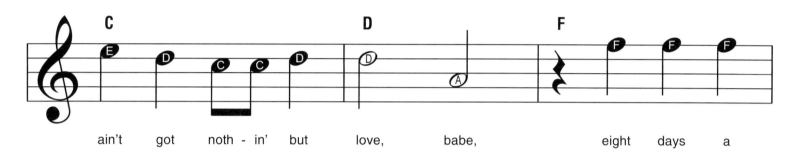

ain't got noth - in' but love, babe, eight days a

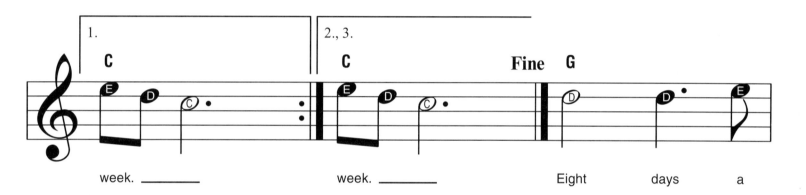

week. _____ week. _____ Eight days a

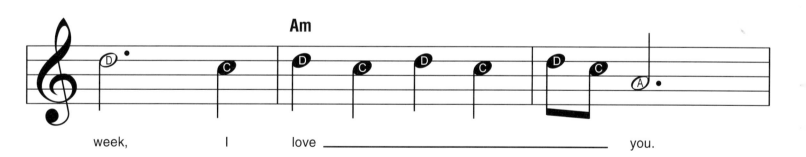

week, I love _____ you.

D.C. al Fine
(Return to beginning
and play to Fine)

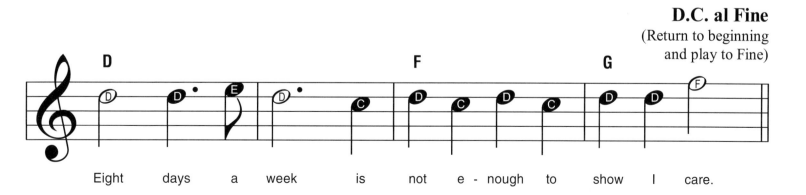

Eight days a week is not e - nough to show I care.

Eleanor Rigby

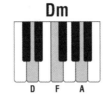

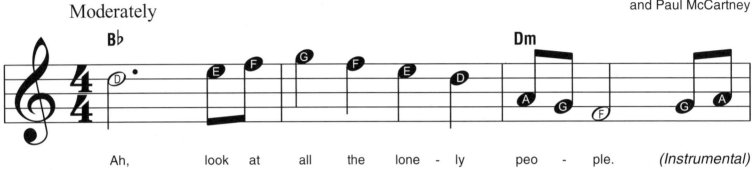

Words and Music by John Lennon
and Paul McCartney

Moderately

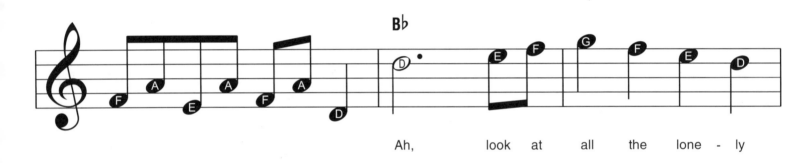

Ah,   look   at   all   the   lone - ly   peo - ple.   *(Instrumental)*

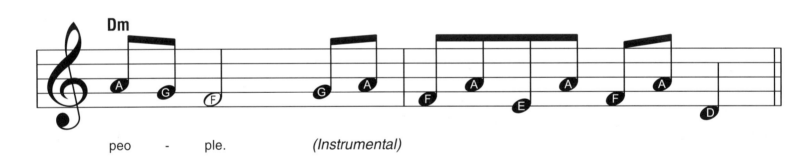

Ah,   look   at   all   the   lone - ly

peo - ple.   *(Instrumental)*

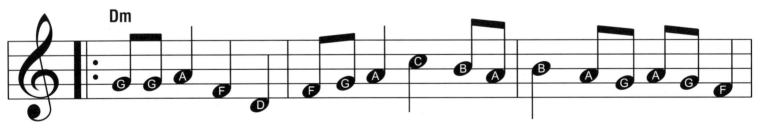

1. El - ea - nor Rig - by   picks   up   the   rice   in   the   church   where   a   wed - ding   has

2., 3. *See additional lyrics*

been. Lives in a dream, ___ waits at the win - dow,

wear - ing a face that she keeps in a jar by the door.

Chorus

Who is it for? ___ All the lone - ly peo - ple, where

do they all come from? All the lone - ly

peo - ple, where do they all be - long? long?

Additional Lyrics

2. Father McKenzie writing the words of a sermon that no one will hear.
   No one comes near.
   Look at him working, darning his socks in the night when there's nobody there.
   What does he care?
   Chorus

3. Eleanor Rigby died in the church and was buried along with her name.
   Nobody came.
   Father McKenzie wiping the dirt from his hands as he walks from the grave.
   No one was saved.
   Chorus

The Fool on the Hill

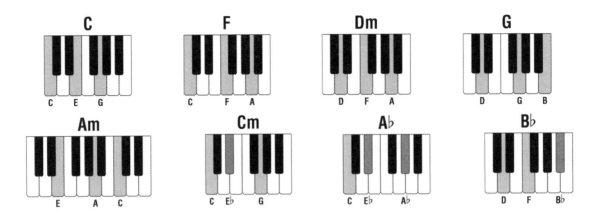

Words and Music by John Lennon
and Paul McCartney

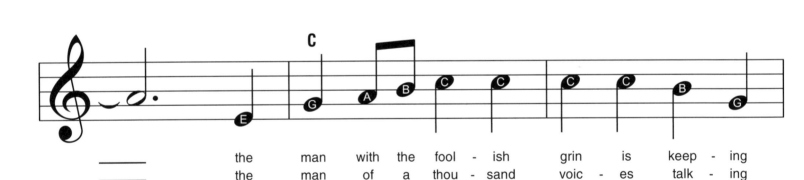

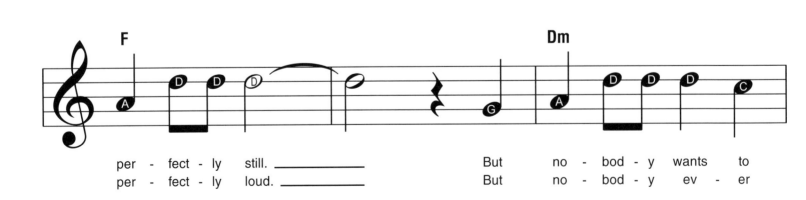

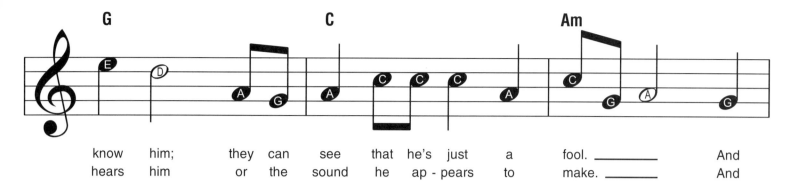

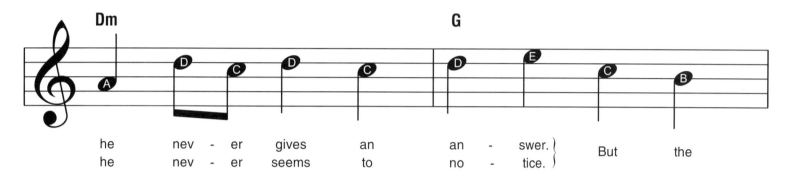

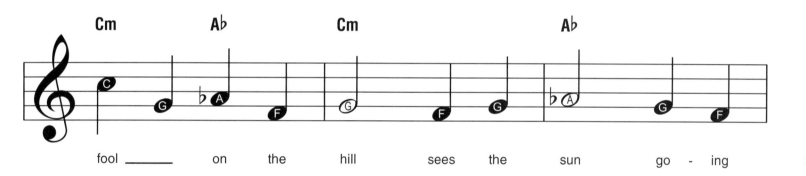

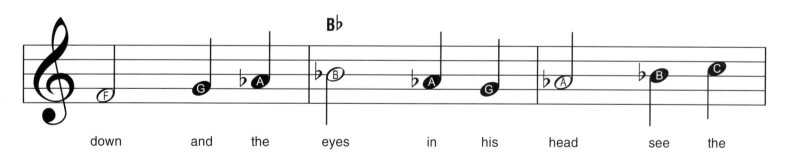

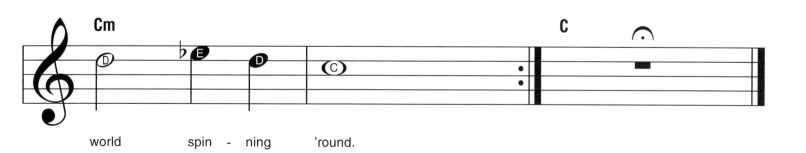

From Me to You

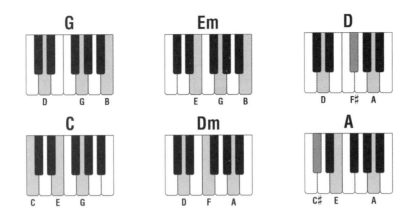

Words and Music by John Lennon
and Paul McCartney

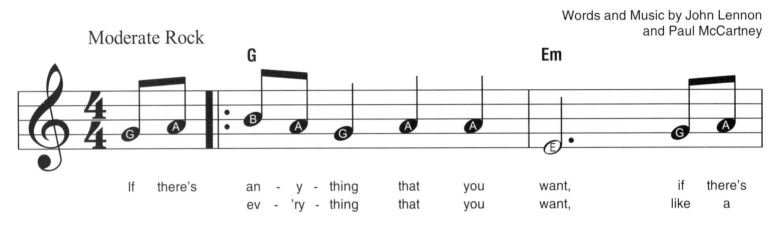

Moderate Rock

If there's an - y - thing that you want, if there's
ev - 'ry - thing that you want, like a

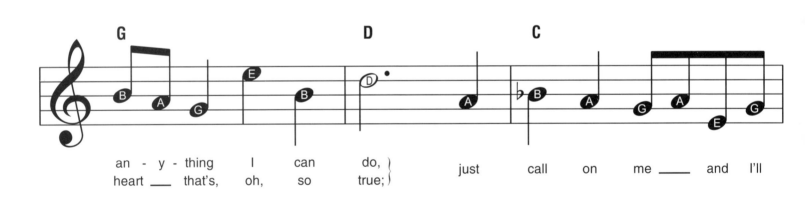

an - y - thing I can do, } just call on me ___ and I'll
heart ___ that's, oh, so true; }

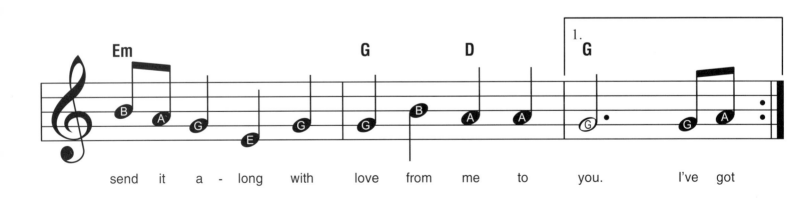

send it a - long with love from me to you. I've got

Get Back

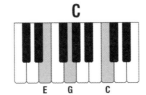

Words and Music by John Lennon
and Paul McCartney

Moderate Rock

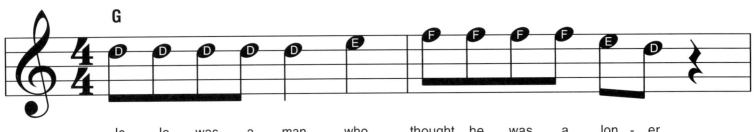

Jo   Jo   was   a   man   who   thought   he   was   a   lon - er,
Sweet   Lo - ret - ta   Mar - tin   thought   she   was   a   wom - an,

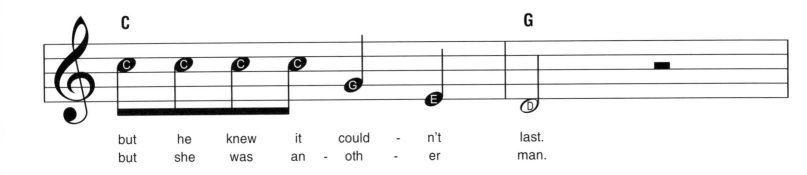

but   he   knew   it   could - n't   last.
but   she   was   an - oth - er   man.

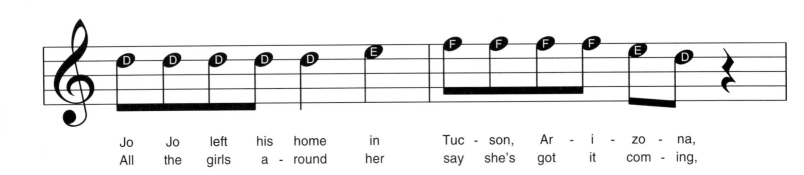

Jo   Jo   left   his   home   in   Tuc - son,   Ar - i - zo - na,
All   the   girls   a - round   her   say   she's   got   it   com - ing,

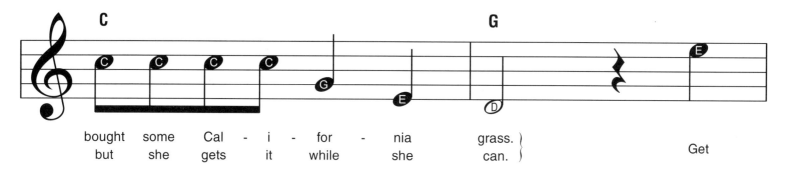

bought some Cal - i - for - nia grass. }
but she gets it while she can. }

Get

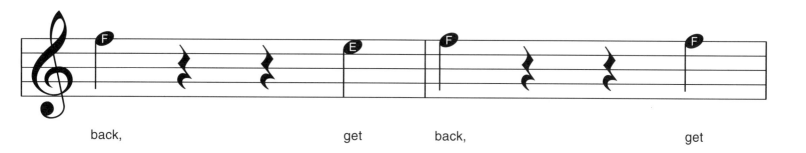

back, get back, get

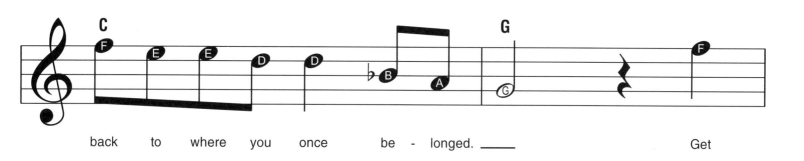

back to where you once be - longed. ____ Get

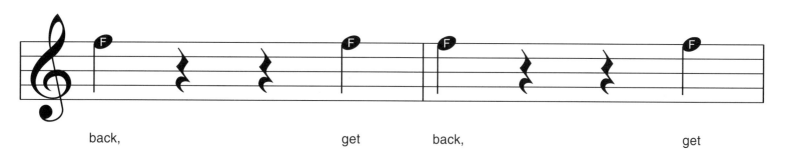

back, get back, get

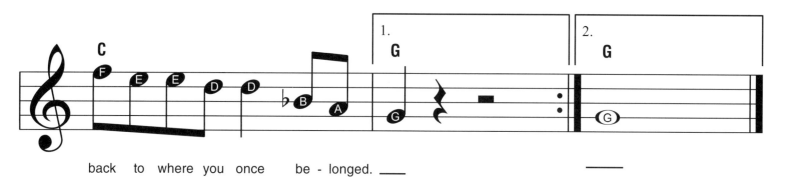

back to where you once be - longed. ___ ___

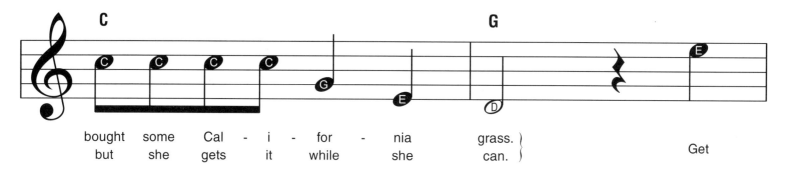

Girl

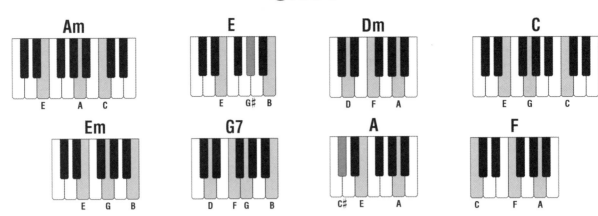

Words and Music by John Lennon
and Paul McCartney

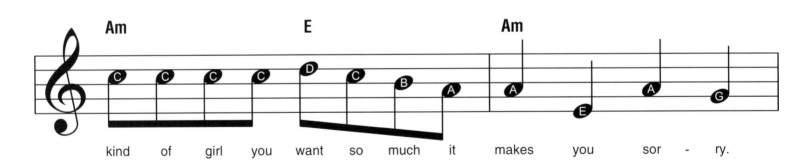

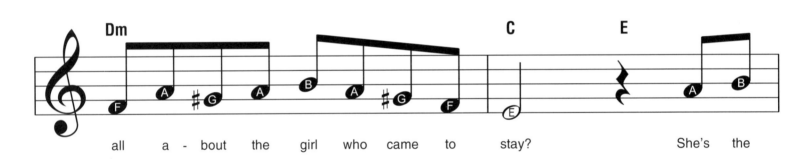

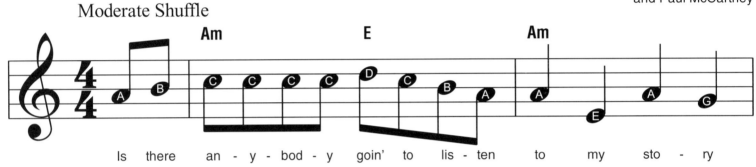

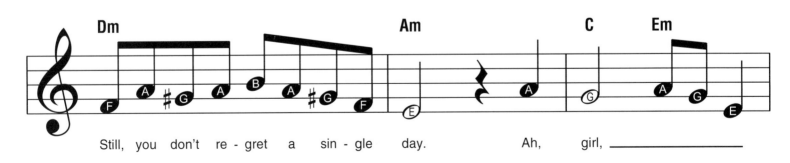

Is there an - y - bod - y goin' to lis - ten to my sto - ry

all a - bout the girl who came to stay? She's the

kind of girl you want so much it makes you sor - ry.

Still, you don't re - gret a sin - gle day. Ah, girl, _____

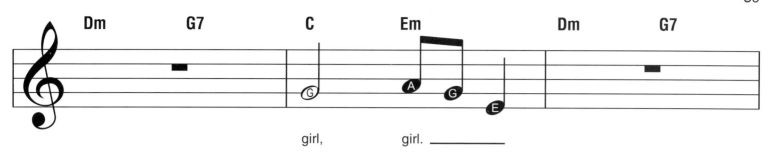

girl,   girl. _____

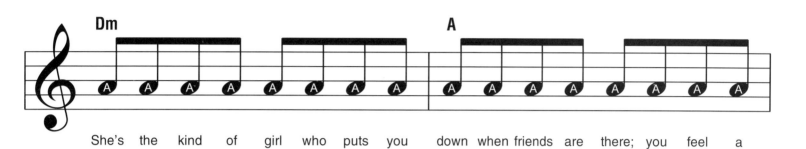

She's the kind of girl who puts you   down when friends are there; you feel a

fool. _____   When you say she's look - ing good, she

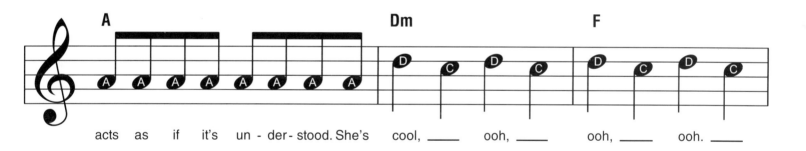

acts as if it's un - der - stood. She's cool, ____ ooh, ____ ooh, ____ ooh. ____

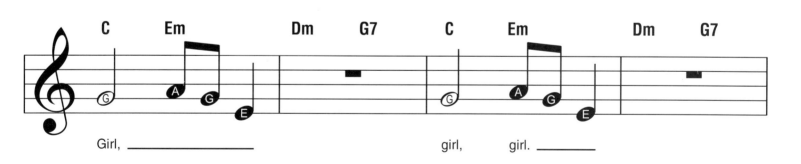

Girl, _____   girl,   girl. _____

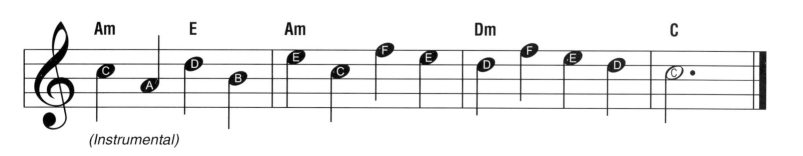

(Instrumental)

Golden Slumbers

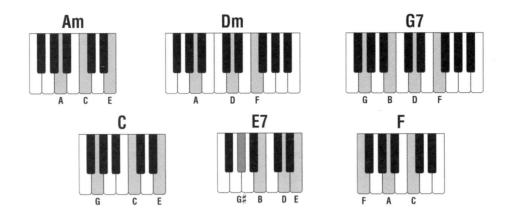

Words and Music by John Lennon
and Paul McCartney

Moderately slow

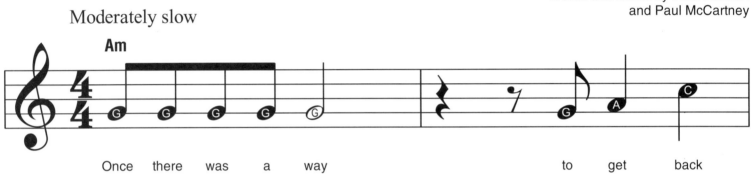

Once there was a way to get back

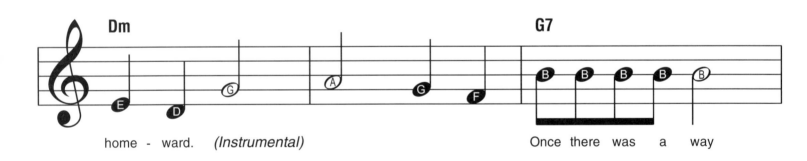

home - ward. *(Instrumental)*   Once there was a way

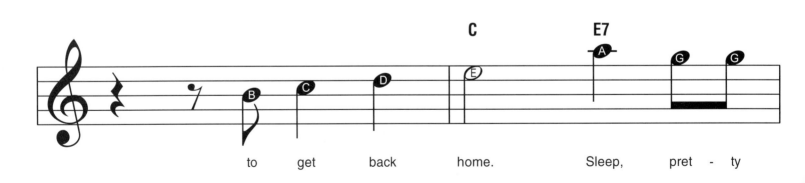

to get back home.   Sleep, pret - ty

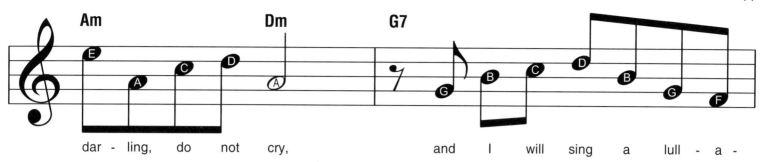

dar - ling, do not cry, and I will sing a lull - a -

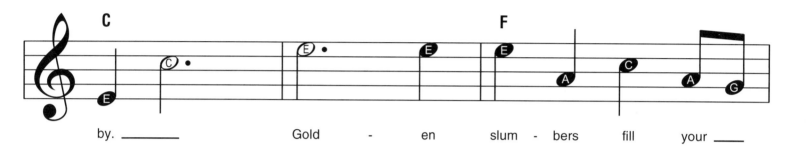

by. _____ Gold - en slum - bers fill your _____

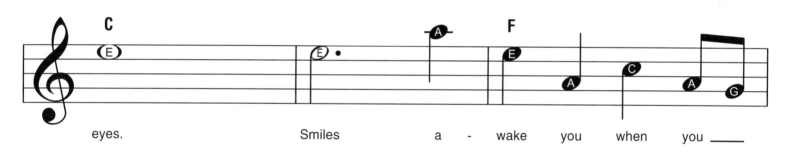

eyes. Smiles a - wake you when you _____

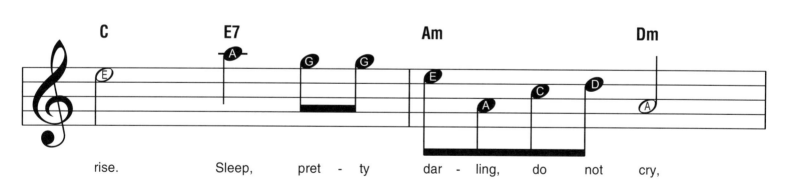

rise. Sleep, pret - ty dar - ling, do not cry,

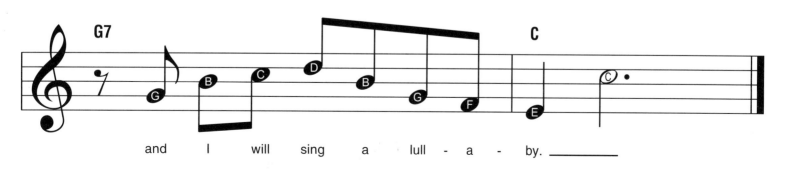

and I will sing a lull - a - by. _____

Good Day Sunshine

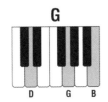
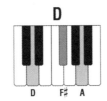
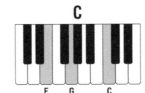
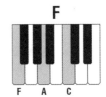

Words and Music by John Lennon
and Paul McCartney

Moderate Shuffle

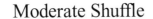

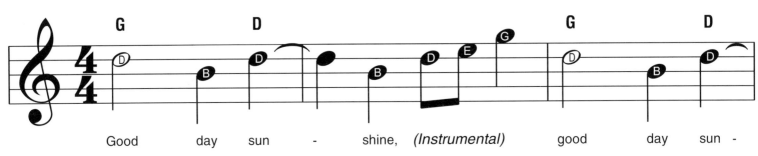

Good day sun - shine, *(Instrumental)* good day sun -

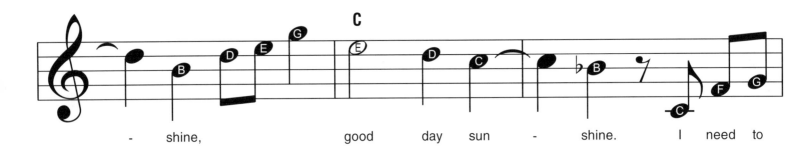

- shine, good day sun - shine. I need to

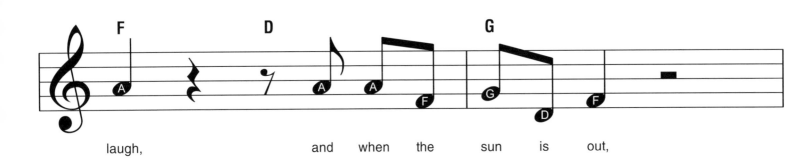

laugh, and when the sun is out,

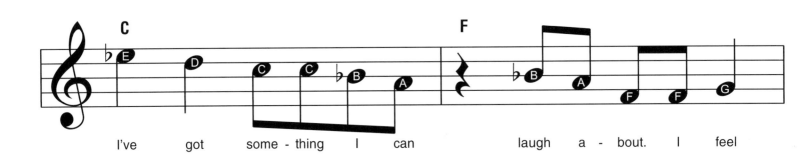

I've got some - thing I can laugh a - bout. I feel

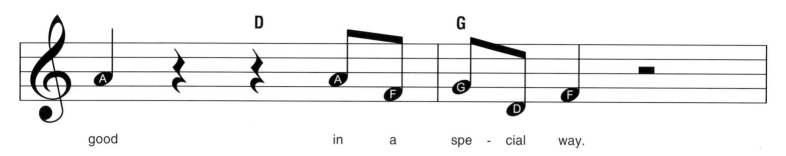

good in a spe - cial way.

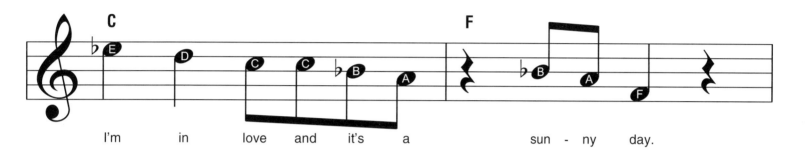

I'm in love and it's a sun - ny day.

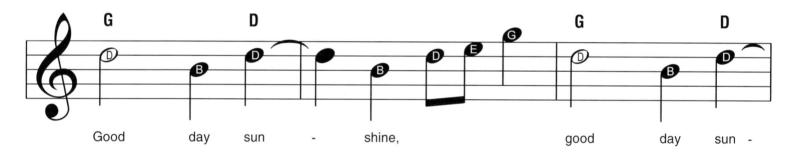

Good day sun - shine, good day sun -

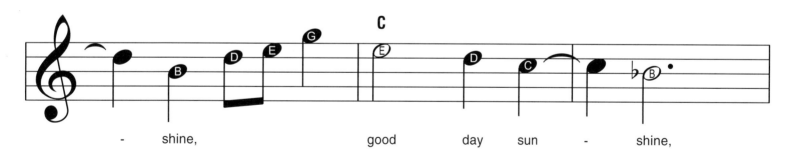

- shine, good day sun - shine,

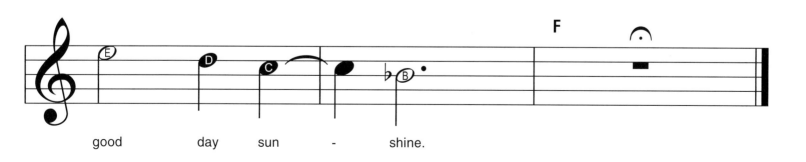

good day sun - shine.

Got to Get You into My Life

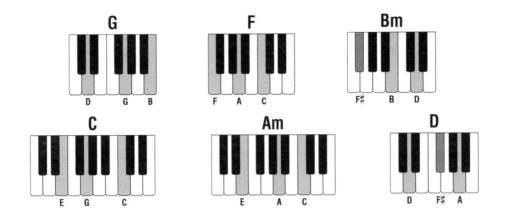

Words and Music by John Lennon
and Paul McCartney

Moderately fast Shuffle

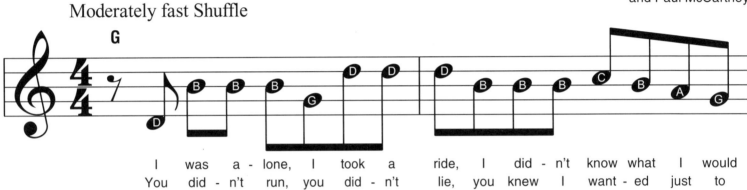

I was a-lone, I took a ride, I did-n't know what I would
You did-n't run, you did-n't lie, you knew I want-ed just to

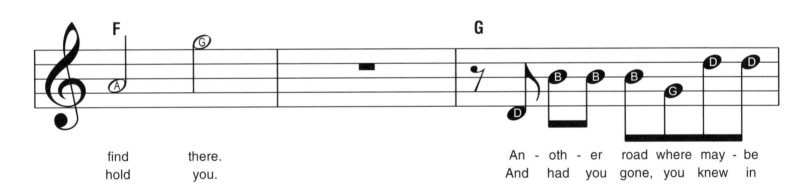

find there.
hold you.

An-oth-er road where may-be
And had you gone, you knew in

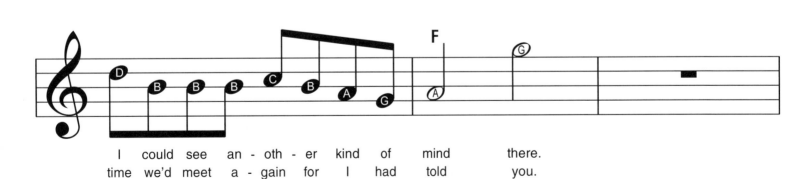

I could see an-oth-er kind of mind there.
time we'd meet a-gain for I had told you.

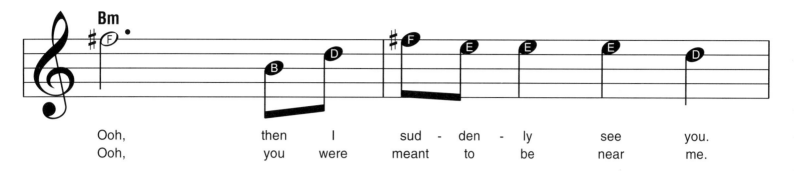

Ooh,   then   I   sud - den - ly   see   you.
Ooh,   you   were   meant   to   be   near   me.

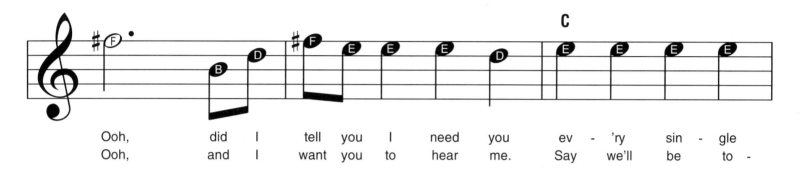

Ooh,   did I   tell you I   need you ev - 'ry sin - gle
Ooh,   and I   want you to hear me. Say we'll be to -

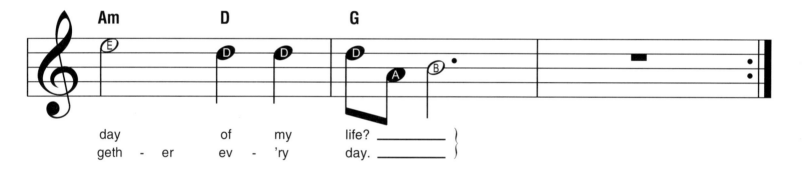

day   of my   life? _____
geth - er ev - 'ry day. _____

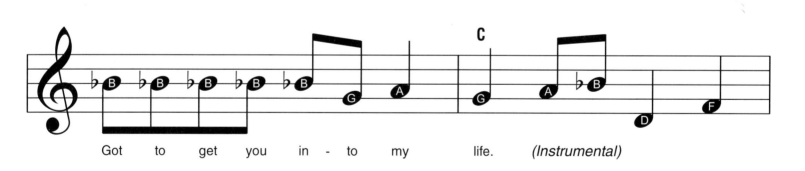

Got to get you in - to my   life.   *(Instrumental)*

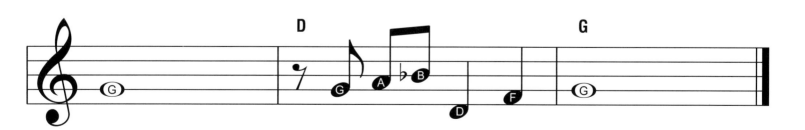

A Hard Day's Night

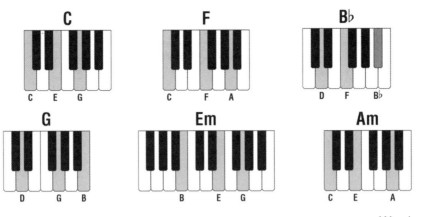

Words and Music by John Lennon
and Paul McCartney

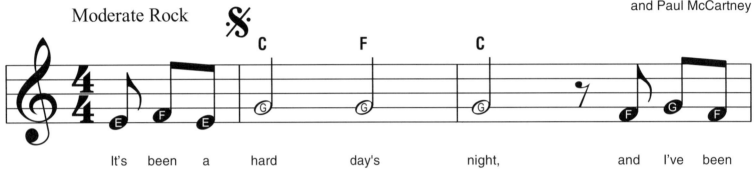

Moderate Rock

It's been a hard day's night, and I've been

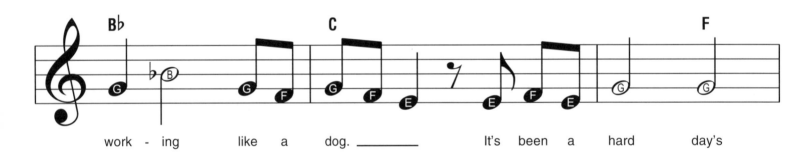

work - ing like a dog. _____ It's been a hard day's

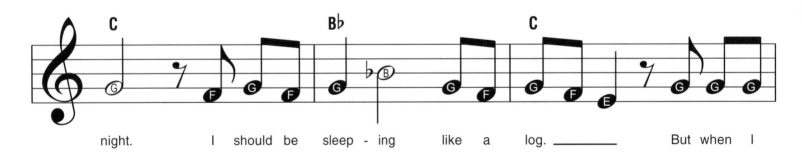

night. I should be sleep - ing like a log. _____ But when I

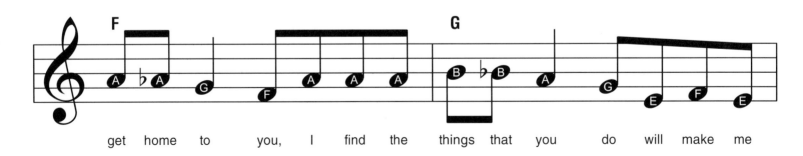

get home to you, I find the things that you do will make me

47

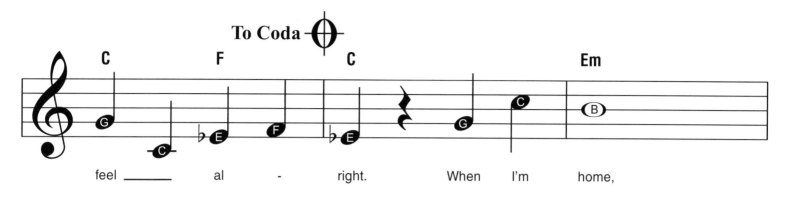

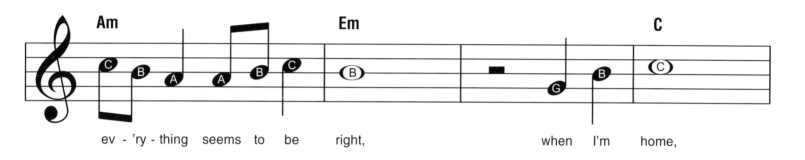

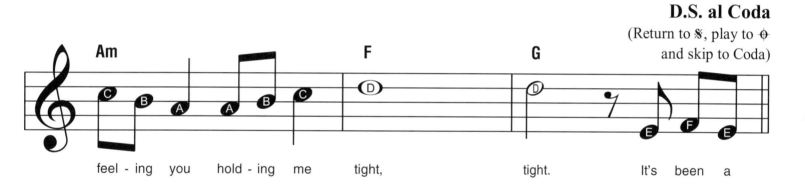

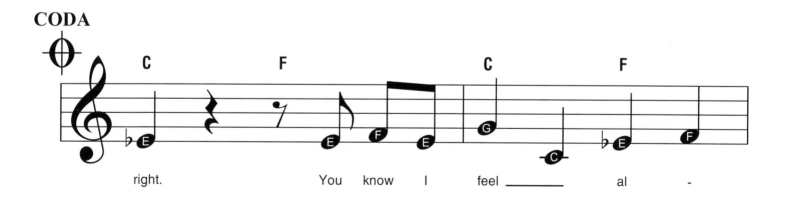

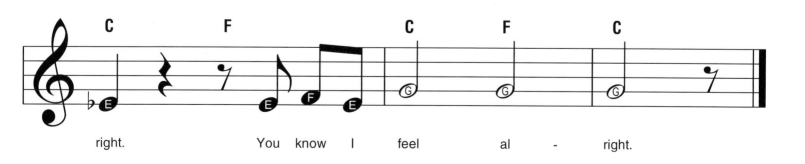

Hello, Goodbye

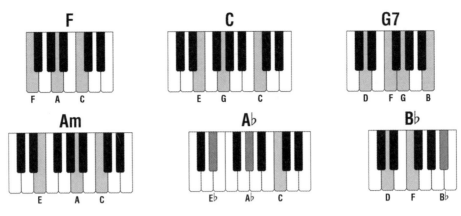

Words and Music by John Lennon
and Paul McCartney

Moderately

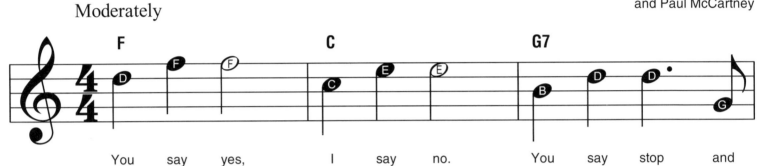

You say yes, I say no. You say stop and

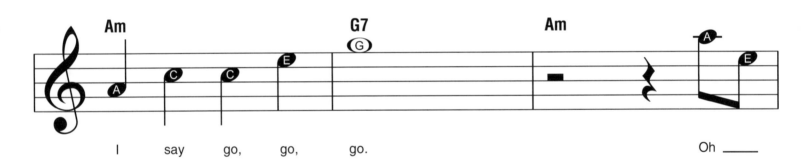

I say go, go, go. Oh ____

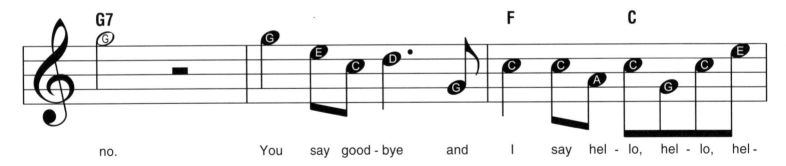

no. You say good - bye and I say hel - lo, hel - lo, hel -

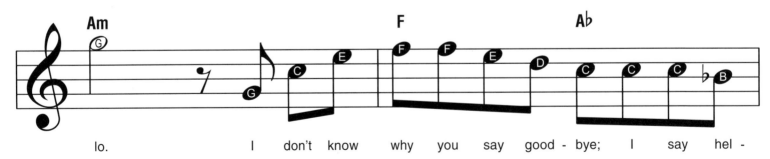

lo. I don't know why you say good bye; I say hel -

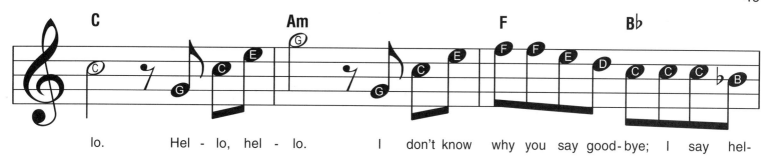

lo.   Hel - lo, hel - lo.   I   don't know   why you say good-bye; I   say hel-

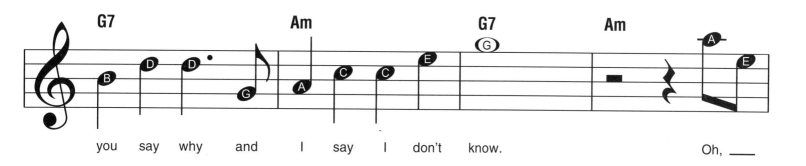

lo.   I   say   high,   you   say   low,

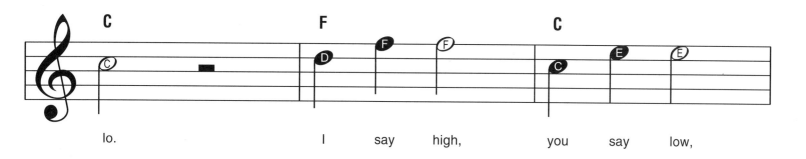

you   say   why   and   I   say   I   don't   know.   Oh, ___

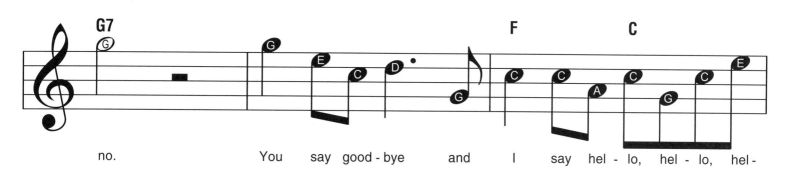

no.   You   say   good-bye   and   I   say hel - lo, hel - lo, hel-

lo.   I   don't   know   why you say good-bye; I   say hel - lo.

Help!

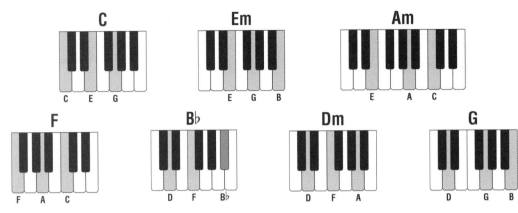

Words and Music by John Lennon
and Paul McCartney

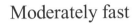
Moderately fast

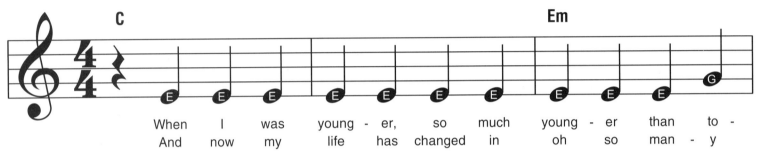

When   I   was   young-er,   so   much   young-er   than   to-
And   now   my   life   has   changed   in   oh   so   man-y

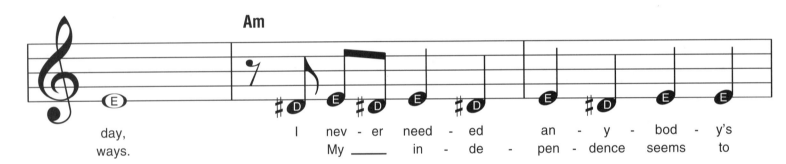

day,   I   nev-er   need-ed   an-y-bod-y's
ways.   My ___ in-de-pen-dence   seems   to

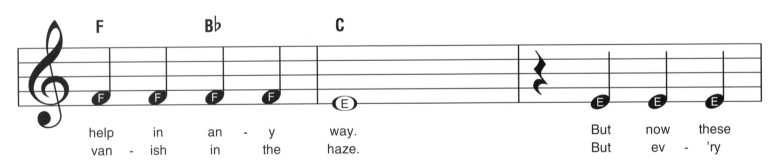

help   in   an-y   way.   But   now   these
van-ish   in   the   haze.   But   ev-'ry

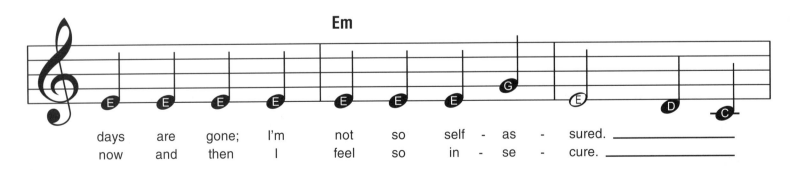

days   are   gone;   I'm   not   so   self-as-sured. ___
now   and   then   I   feel   so   in-se-cure. ___

Here Comes the Sun

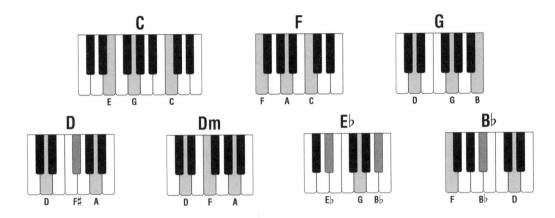

Words and Music by
George Harrison

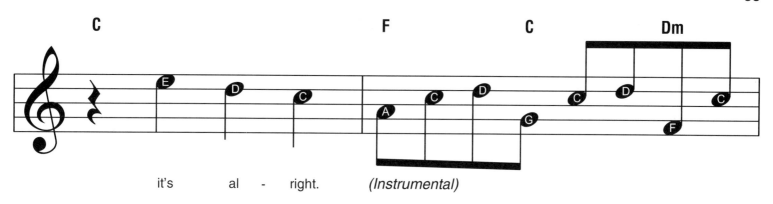

it's al - right. *(Instrumental)*

To Coda

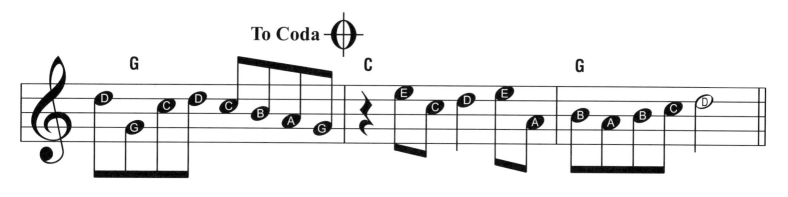

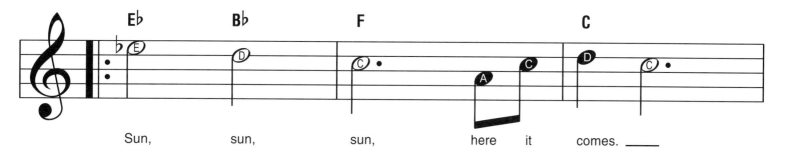

Sun, sun, sun, here it comes. _____

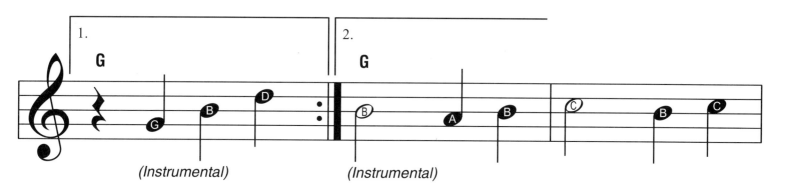

(Instrumental) *(Instrumental)*

D.C. al Coda
(Return to beginning,
play to ⊕ and skip to Coda)

CODA

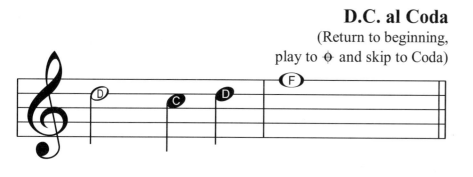

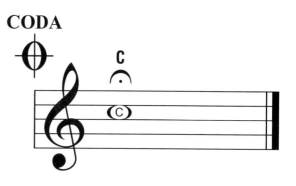

Here, There and Everywhere

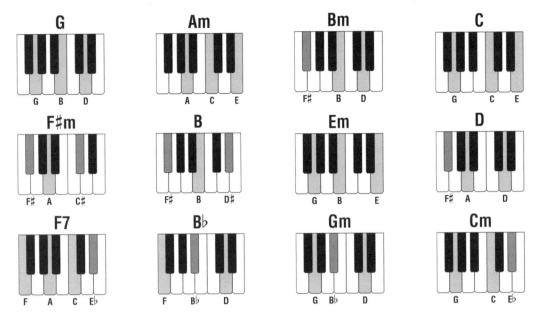

Words and Music by John Lennon
and Paul McCartney

Moderately

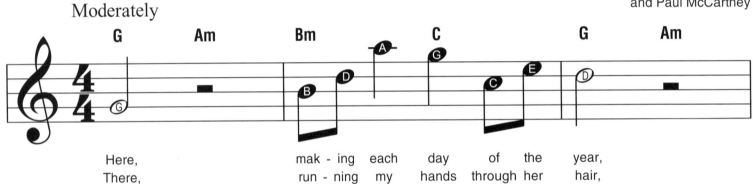

Here,
There,

mak - ing each day of the year,
run - ning my hands through her hair,

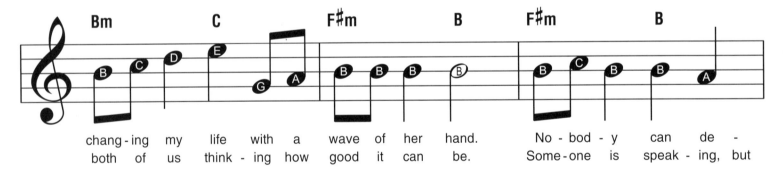

chang - ing my life with a wave of her hand.
both of us think - ing how good it can be.

No - bod - y can de -
Some - one is speak - ing, but

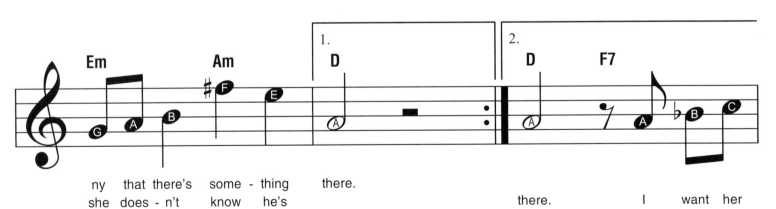

ny that there's some - thing there.
she does - n't know he's

there. I want her

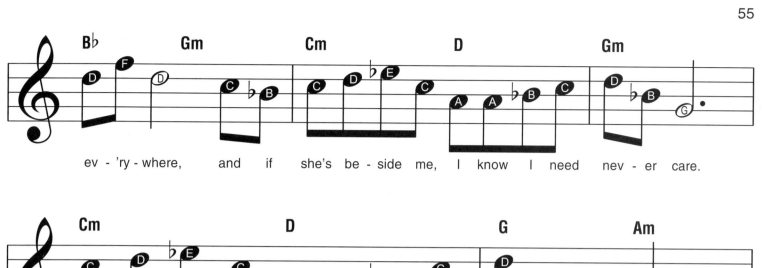

ev - 'ry - where, and if she's be - side me, I know I need nev - er care.

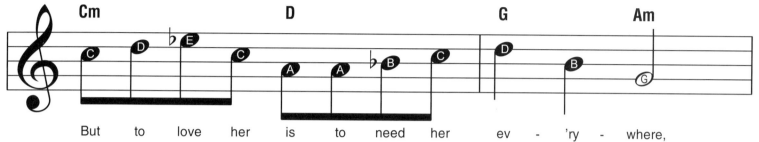

But to love her is to need her ev - 'ry - where,

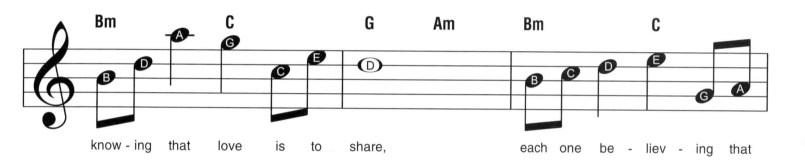

know - ing that love is to share, each one be - liev - ing that

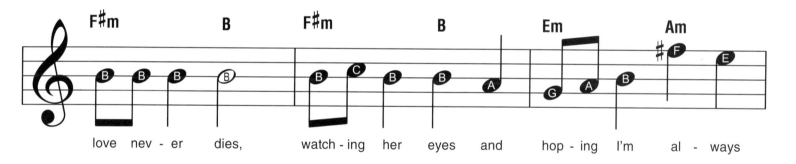

love nev - er dies, watch - ing her eyes and hop - ing I'm al - ways

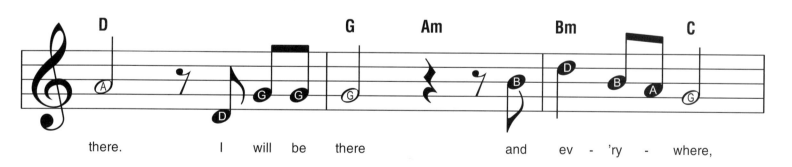

there. I will be there and ev - 'ry - where,

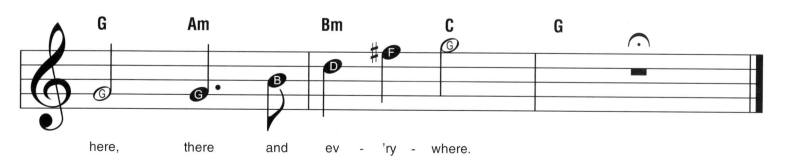

here, there and ev - 'ry - where.

Hey Jude

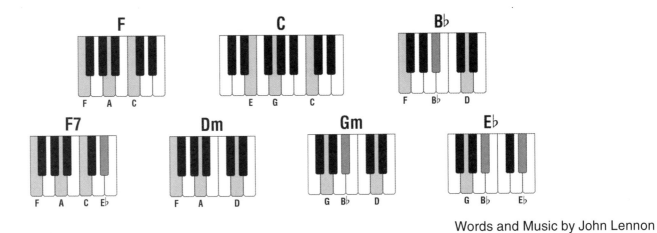

Words and Music by John Lennon
and Paul McCartney

Moderately

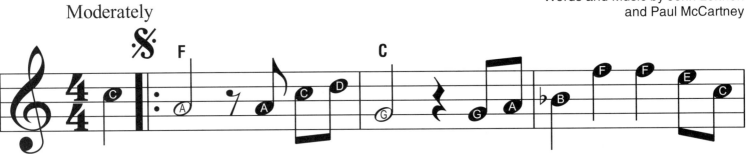

1. Hey Jude, don't make it bad. Take a sad song and make it
(2., 3.) *See additional lyrics*

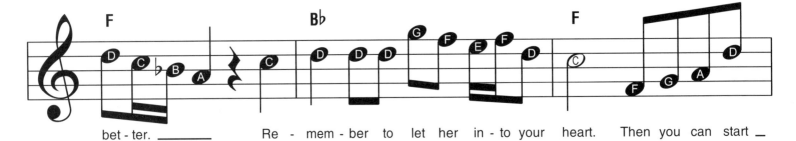

bet - ter. _____ Re - mem - ber to let her in - to your heart. Then you can start _

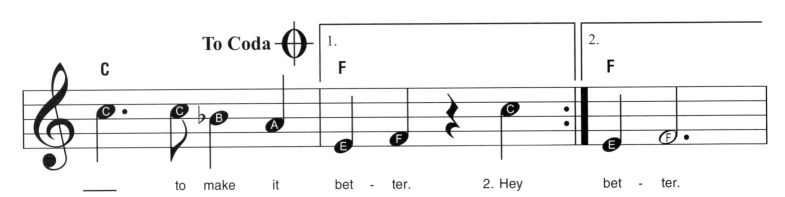

_ to make it bet - ter. 2. Hey bet - ter.

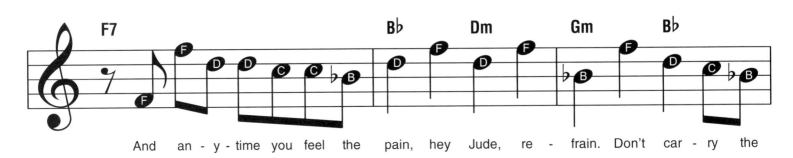

And an - y - time you feel the pain, hey Jude, re - frain. Don't car - ry the

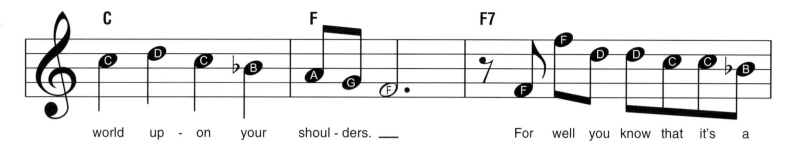

world up - on your shoul - ders. ___ For well you know that it's a

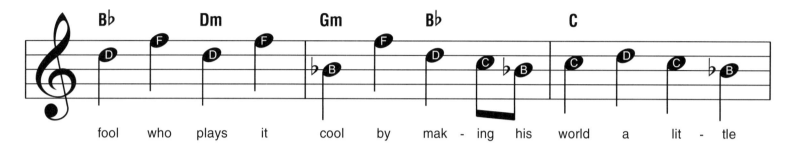

fool who plays it cool by mak - ing his world a lit - tle

D.S. al Coda
(Return to 𝄋, play to ⊕
and skip to Coda)

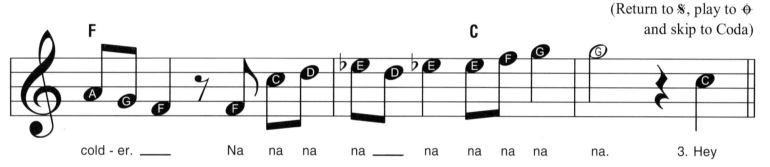

cold - er. ___ Na na na na ___ na na na na na. 3. Hey

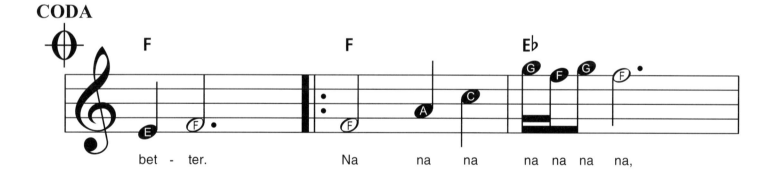

bet - ter. Na na na na na na na,

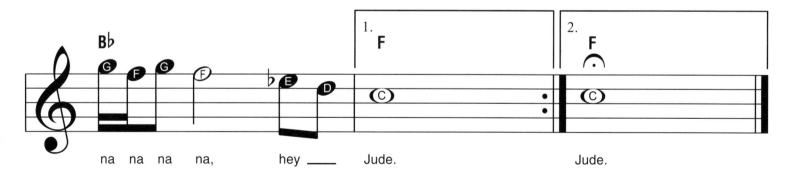

na na na na, hey ___ Jude. Jude.

Additional Lyrics

2. Hey Jude, don't be afraid.
   You were made to go out and get her.
   The minute you let her under your skin,
   Then you begin to make it better.

3. Hey Jude, don't let me down.
   You have found her, now go and get her.
   Remember to let her into your heart,
   Then you can start to make it better.

I Feel Fine

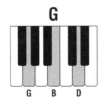
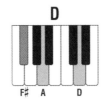
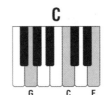
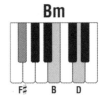

Words and Music by John Lennon
and Paul McCartney

Moderately bright

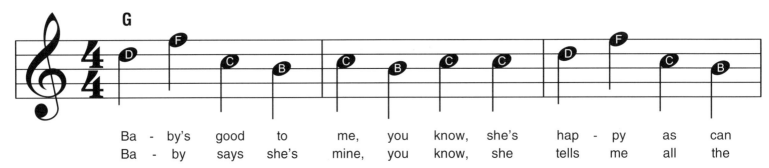

Ba - by's good to me, you know, she's hap - py as can
Ba - by says she's mine, you know, she tells me all the

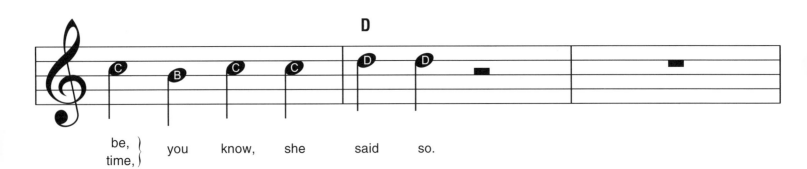

be, } you know, she said so.
time, }

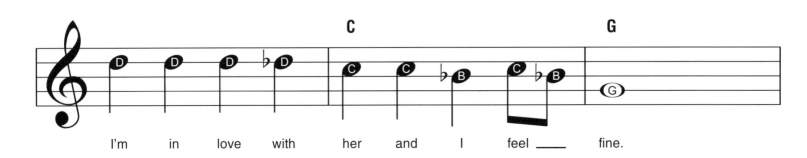

I'm in love with her and I feel ____ fine.

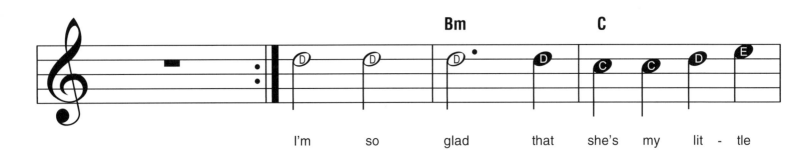

I'm so glad that she's my lit - tle

I Saw Her Standing There

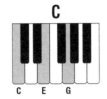
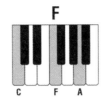
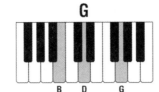
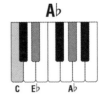

Words and Music by John Lennon
and Paul McCartney

Brightly

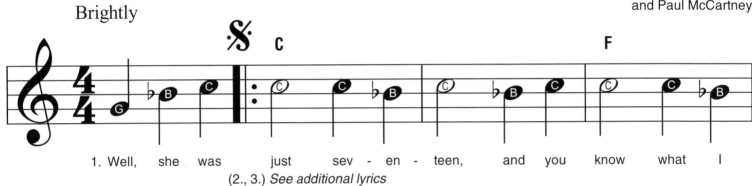

1. Well, she was just sev - en - teen, and you know what I
(2., 3.) *See additional lyrics*

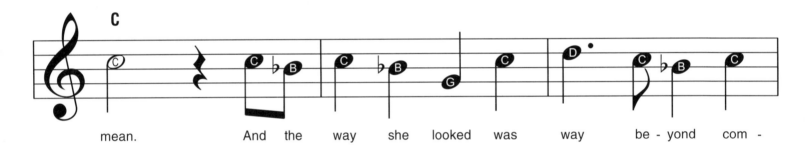

mean. And the way she looked was way be - yond com -

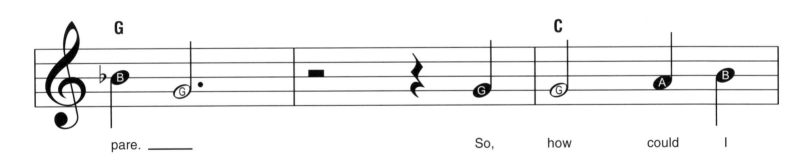

pare. _____ So, how could I

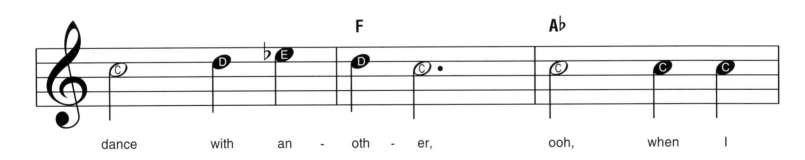

dance with an - oth - er, ooh, when I

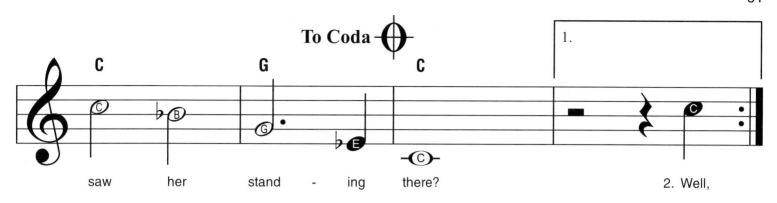

saw her stand - ing there? 2. Well,

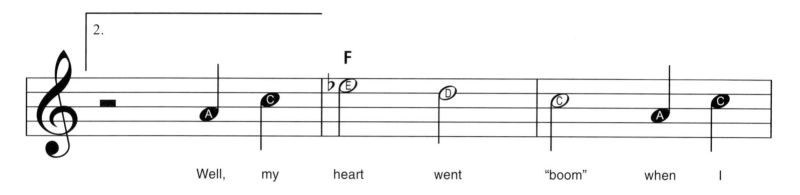

Well, my heart went "boom" when I

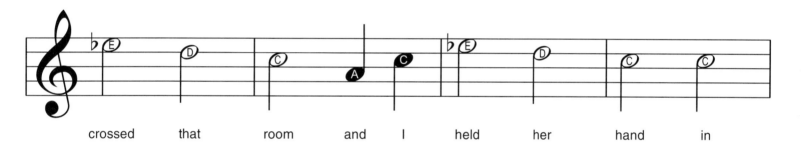

crossed that room and I held her hand in

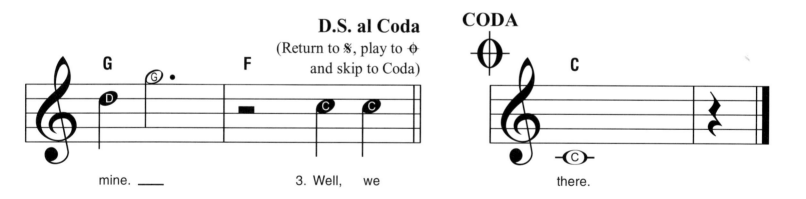

mine. 3. Well, we there.

Additional Lyrics

2. Well, she looked at me, and I, I could see
That before too long, I'd fall in love with her.
She wouldn't dance with another, ooh,
When I saw her standing there.

3. Well, we danced through the night
And we held each other tight,
And before too long, I fell in love with her.
Now, I'll never dance with another, ooh,
Since I saw her standing there.

I Should Have Known Better

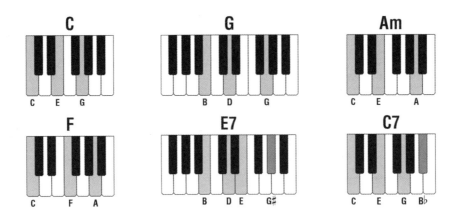

Words and Music by John Lennon
and Paul McCartney

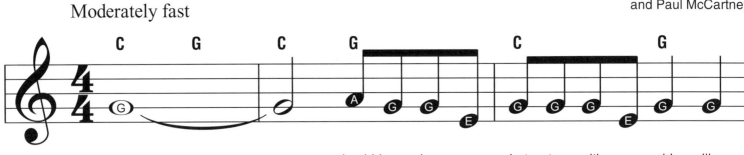

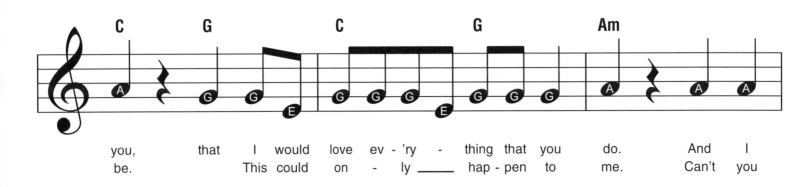

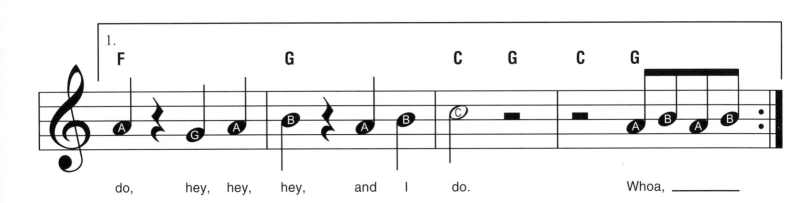

I Want to Hold Your Hand

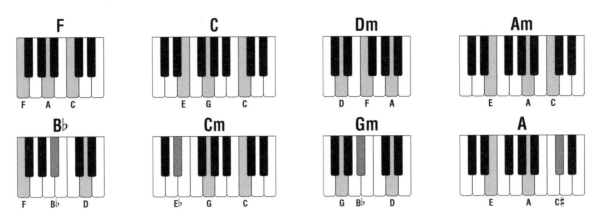

Words and Music by John Lennon
and Paul McCartney

Moderately fast

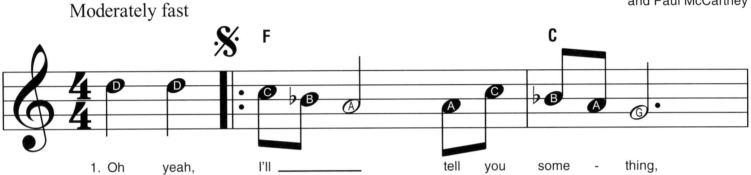

1. Oh yeah, I'll _____ tell you some - thing,
(2., 3.) *See additional lyrics*

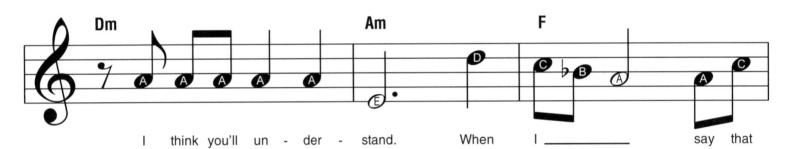

I think you'll un - der - stand. When I _____ say that

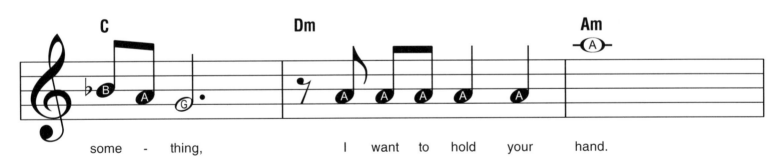

some - thing, I want to hold your hand.

To Coda

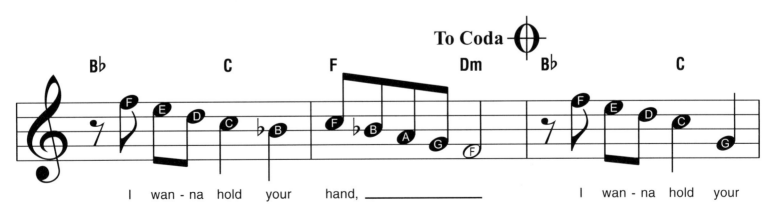

I wan - na hold your hand, _____ I wan - na hold your

Additional Lyrics

2. Oh, please say to me
   You'll let me be your man.
   And please say to me
   You'll let me hold your hand.
   Now let me hold your hand.
   I wanna hold your hand.

3. Yeah, you got that something.
   I think you'll understand.
   When I say that something,
   I wanna hold your hand.
   I wanna hold your hand.
   I wanna hold your hand.

I Will

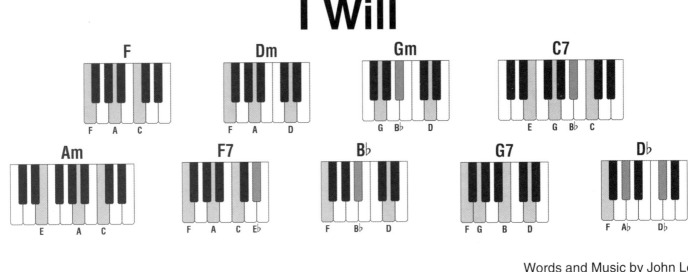

Words and Music by John Lennon
and Paul McCartney

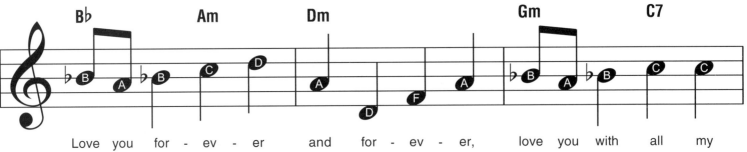

I'll Follow the Sun

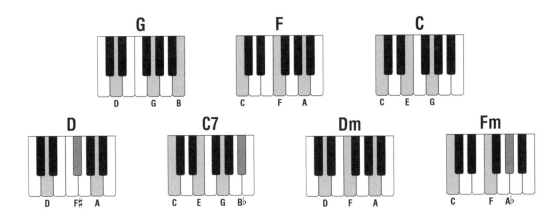

Words and Music by John Lennon
and Paul McCartney

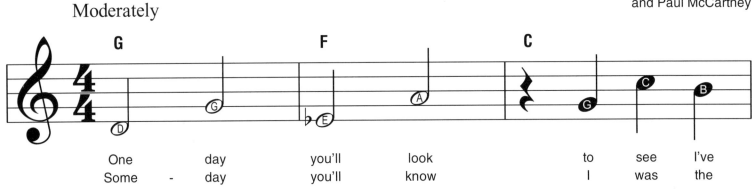

One day   you'll   look   to   see   I've
Some - day you'll   know   I   was   the

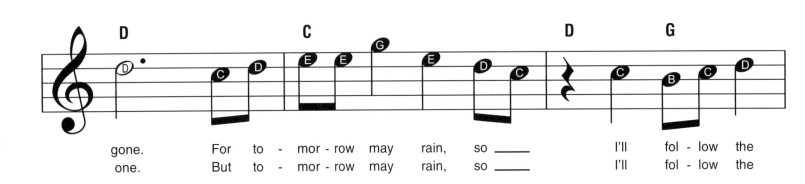

gone.   For to - mor - row may   rain, so ____   I'll   fol - low   the
one.   But to - mor - row may   rain, so ____   I'll   fol - low   the

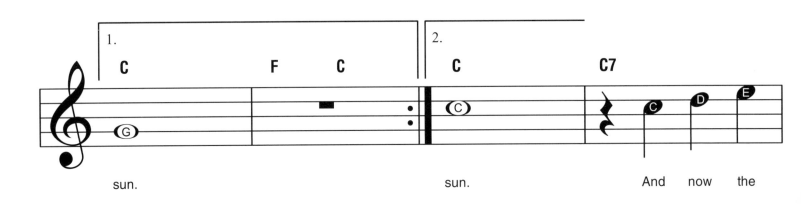

sun.   sun.   And   now   the

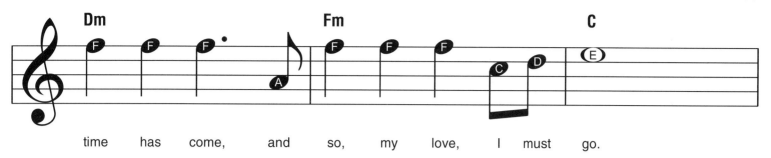

time has come, and so, my love, I must go.

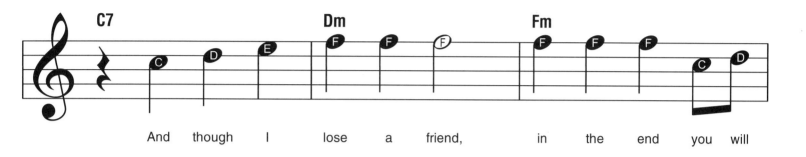

And though I lose a friend, in the end you will

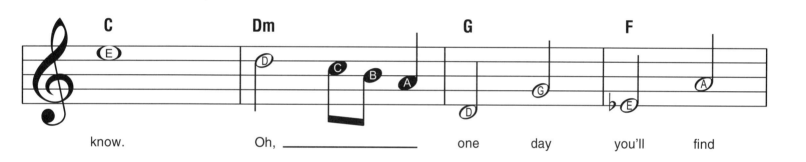

know. Oh, _____ one day you'll find

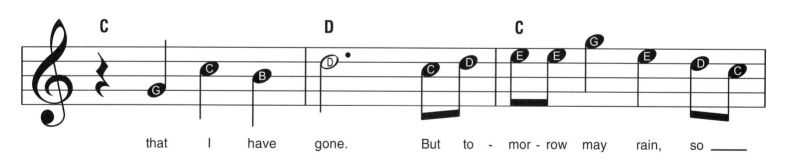

that I have gone. But to - mor - row may rain, so ____

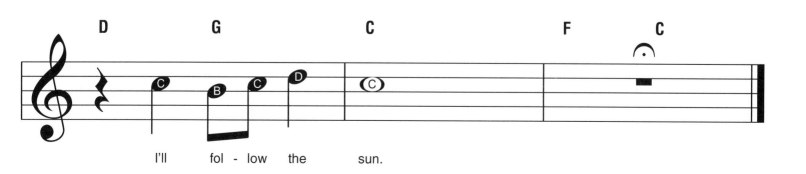

I'll fol - low the sun.

If I Fell

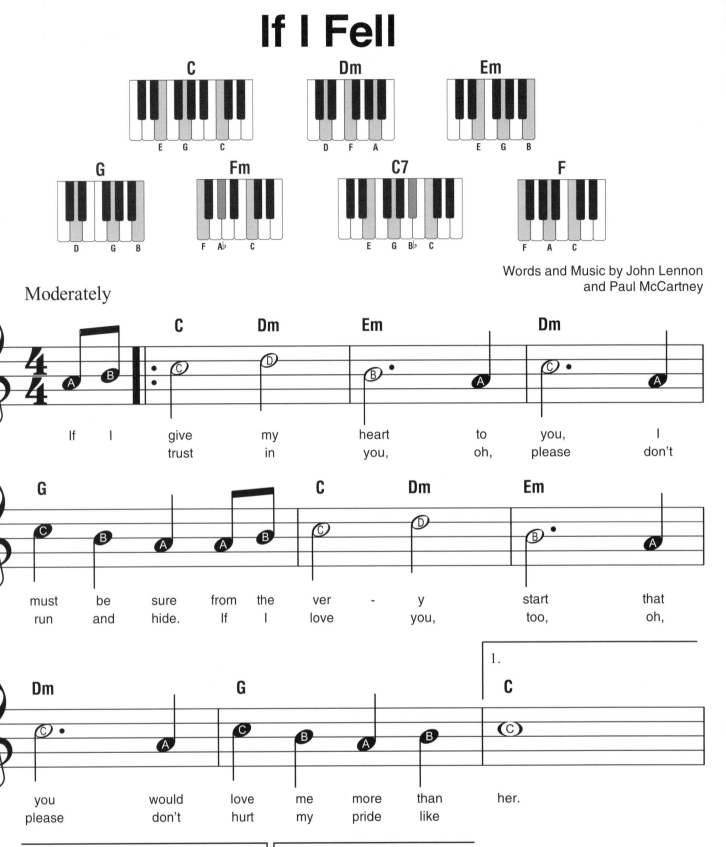

Words and Music by John Lennon
and Paul McCartney

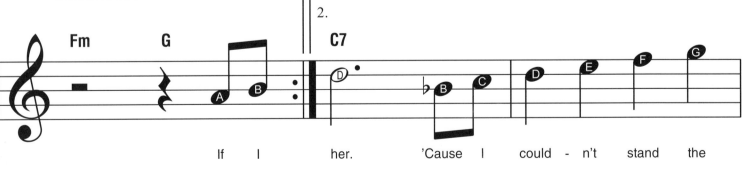

In My Life

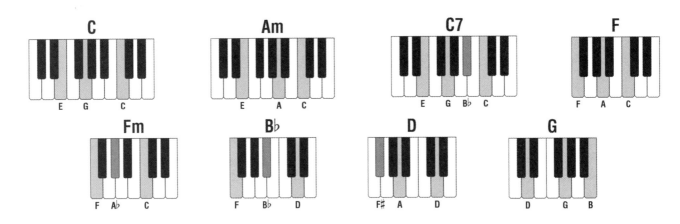

Words and Music by John Lennon
and Paul McCartney

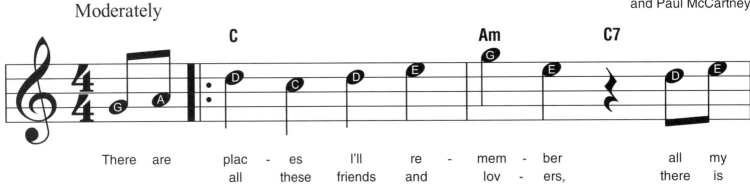

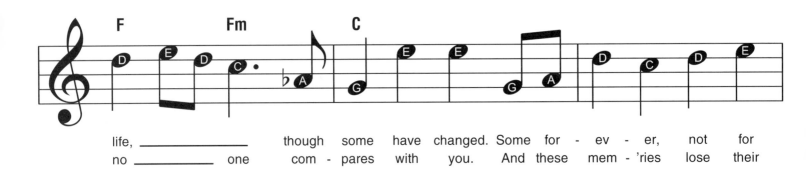

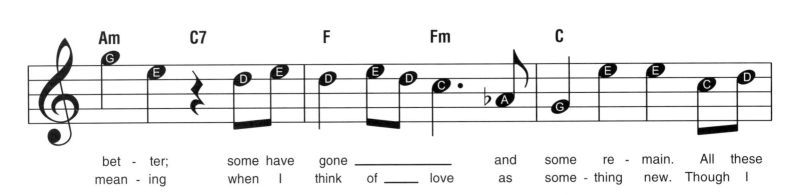

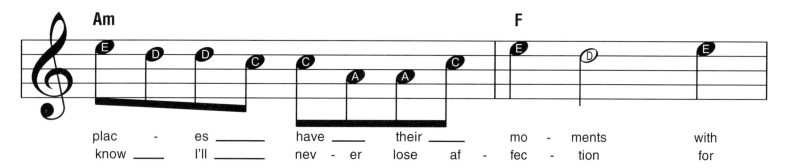

plac - es _____ have _____ their _____ mo - ments with
know _____ I'll _____ nev - er lose af - fec - tion for

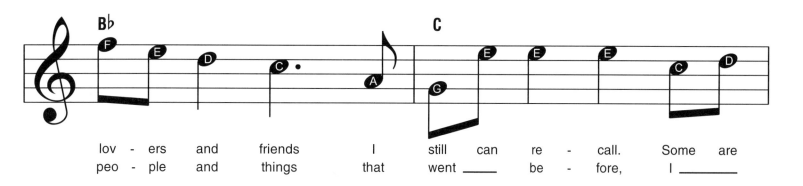

lov - ers and friends I still can re - call. Some are
peo - ple and things that went _____ be - fore, I _____

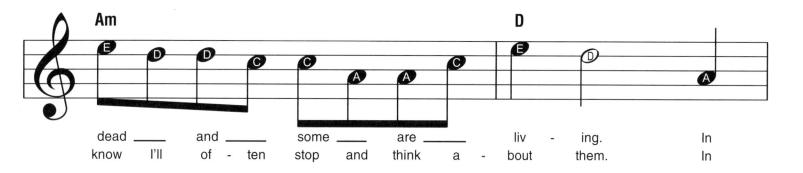

dead _____ and _____ some _____ are _____ liv - ing. In
know I'll of - ten stop and think a - bout them. In

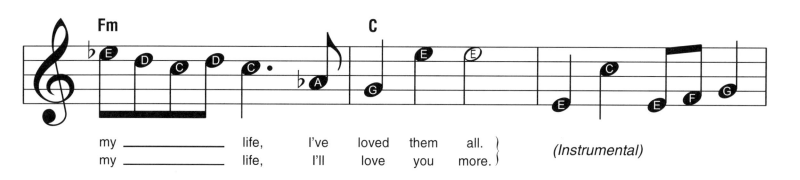

my _____ life, I've loved them all. ⎫
my _____ life, I'll love you more. ⎭ *(Instrumental)*

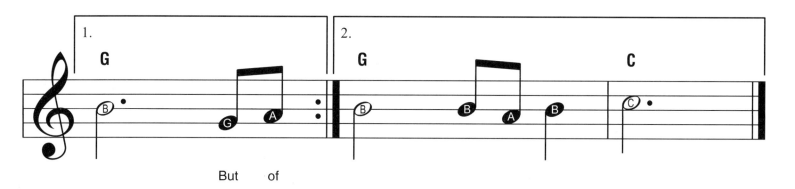

But of

Lady Madonna

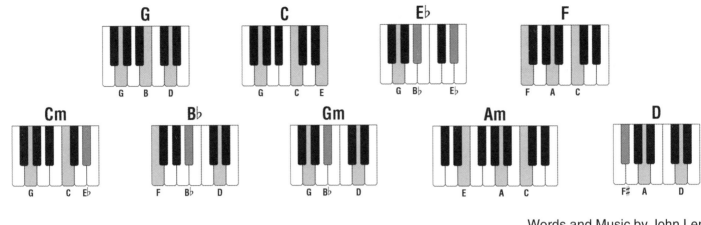

Words and Music by John Lennon
and Paul McCartney

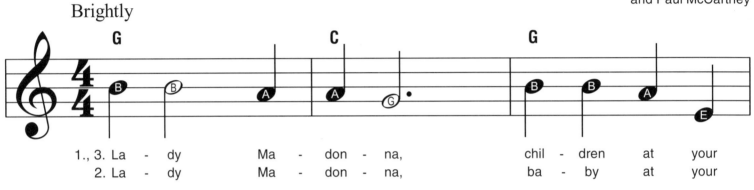

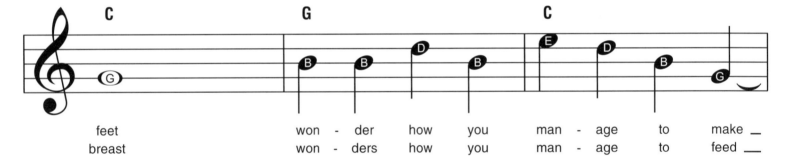

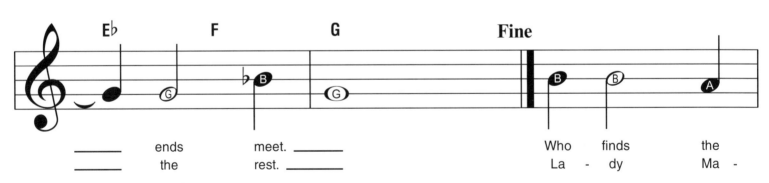

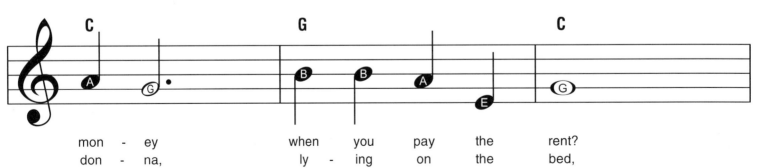

Let It Be

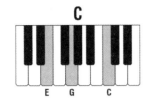
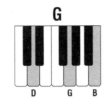
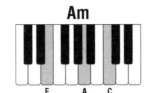
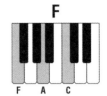

Words and Music by John Lennon
and Paul McCartney

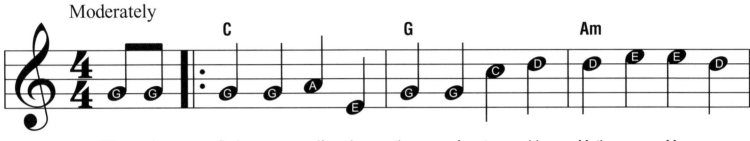

When I find my-self in times of trou-ble, Moth-er Mar-y
when the bro-ken- heart- ed peo- ple liv- ing in the

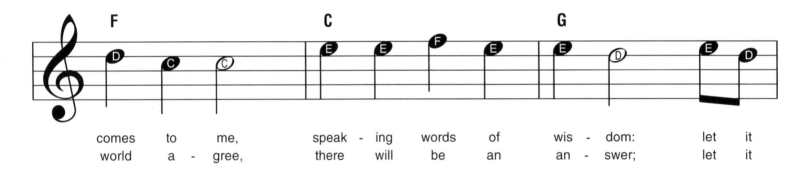

comes to me, speak- ing words of wis- dom: let it
world a - gree, there will be an an - swer; let it

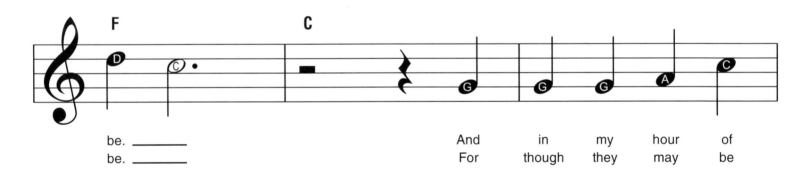

be. _____ And in my hour of
be. _____ For though they may be

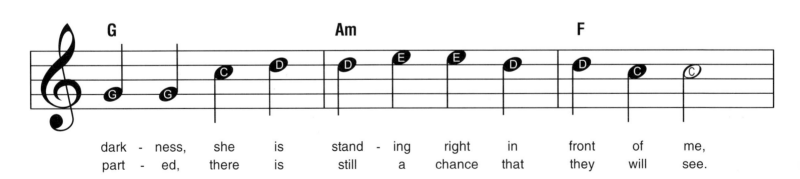

dark- ness, she is stand- ing right in front of me,
part- ed, there is still a chance that they will see.

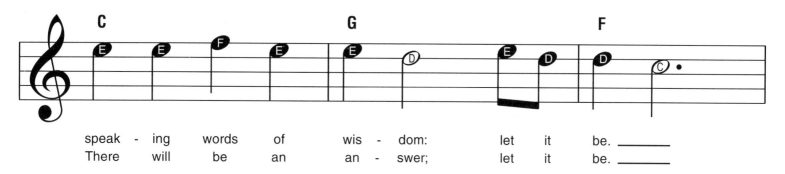

speak - ing words of wis - dom: let it be. _____
There will be an an - swer; let it be. _____

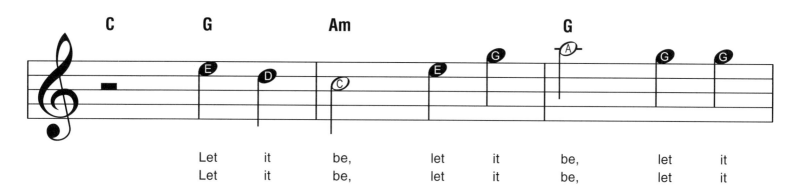

Let it be, let it be, let it
Let it be, let it be, let it

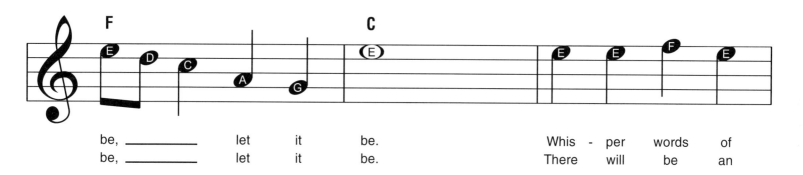

be, _____ let it be. Whis - per words of
be, _____ let it be. There will be an

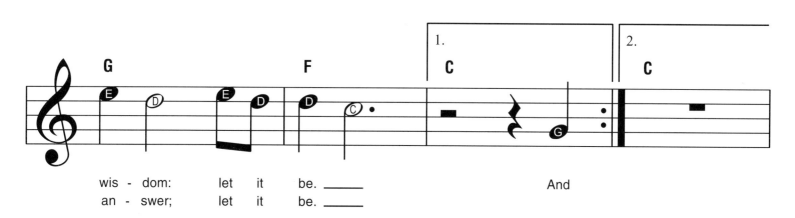

1.
2.

wis - dom: let it be. _____ And
an - swer; let it be. _____

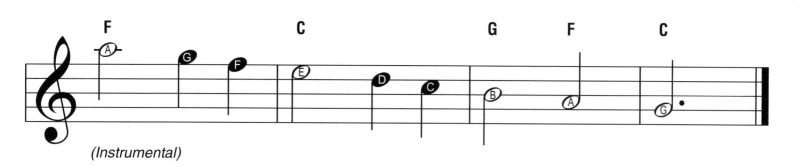

(Instrumental)

The Long and Winding Road

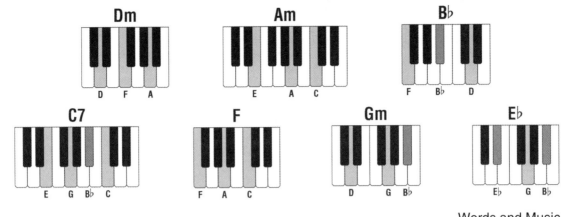

Words and Music by John Lennon
and Paul McCartney

Moderately slow

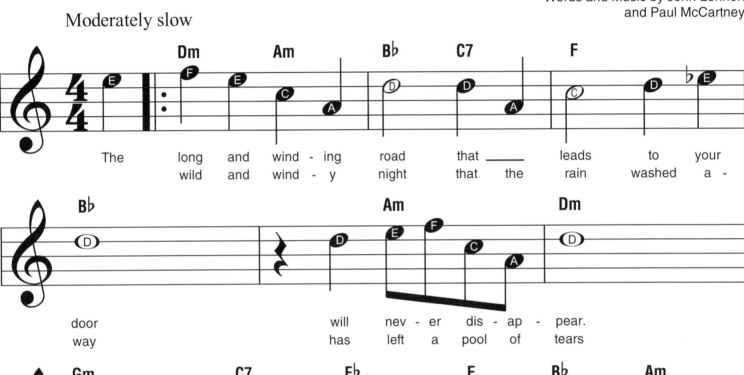

The long and wind - ing road that _____ leads to your
wild and wind - y night that the rain washed a -

door will nev - er dis - ap - pear.
way has left a pool of tears

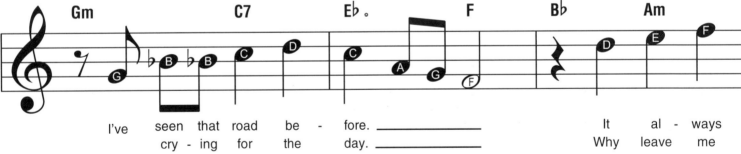

I've seen that road be - fore. _____ It al - ways
cry - ing for the day. _____ Why leave me

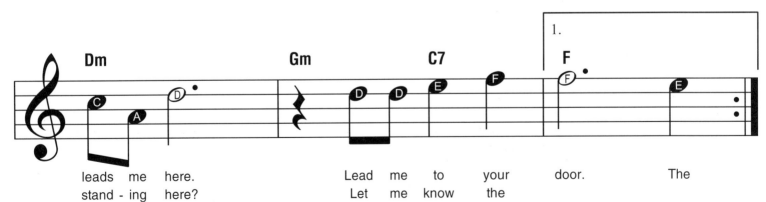

leads me here. Lead me to your door. The
stand - ing here? Let me know the

Love Me Do

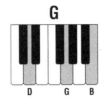
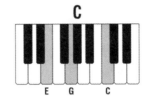
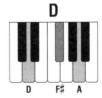

Words and Music by John Lennon
and Paul McCartney

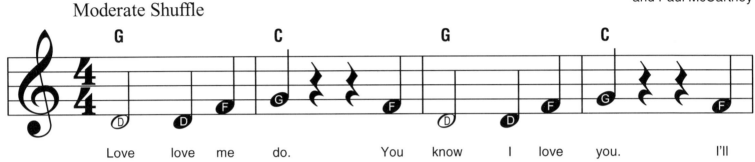

Love love me do. You know I love you. I'll

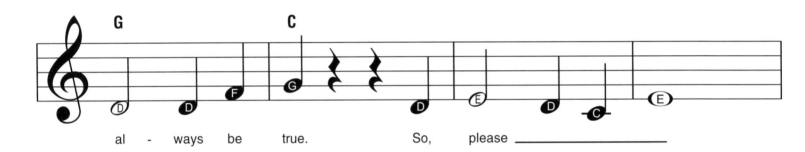

al - ways be true. So, please _____

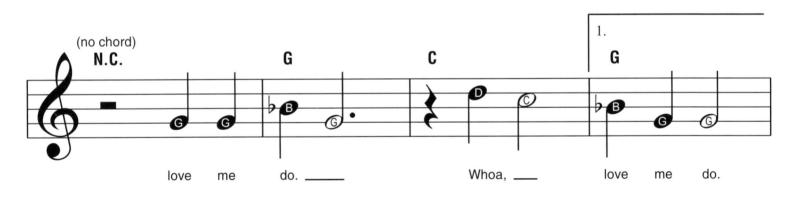

love me do. _____ Whoa, ___ love me do.

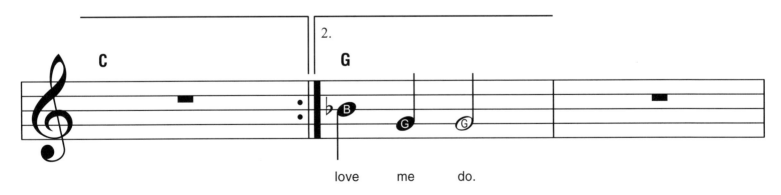

love me do.

Lucy in the Sky with Diamonds

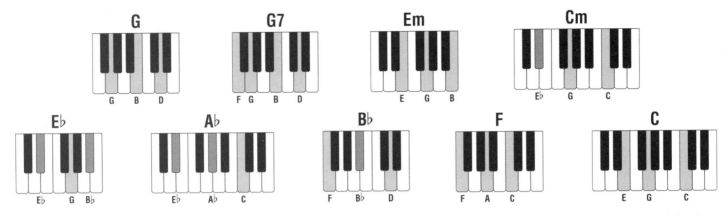

Words and Music by John Lennon
and Paul McCartney

Moderately

Pic - ture your - self in a boat on a riv - er with

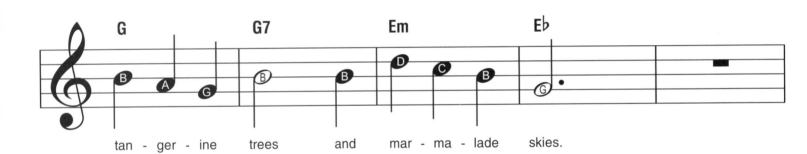

tan - ger - ine trees and mar - ma - lade skies.

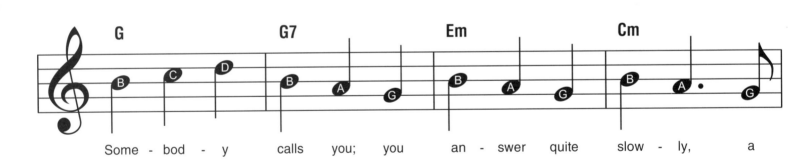

Some - bod - y calls you; you an - swer quite slow - ly, a

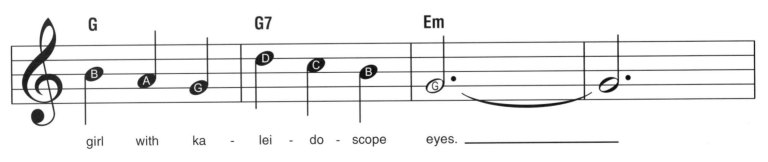

girl with ka - lei - do - scope eyes. _____

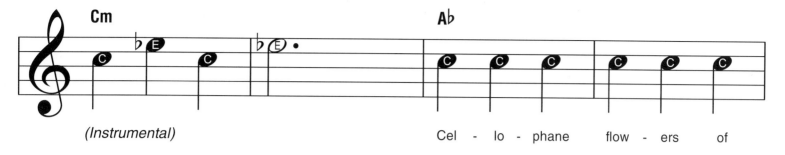

(Instrumental) Cel - lo - phane flow - ers of

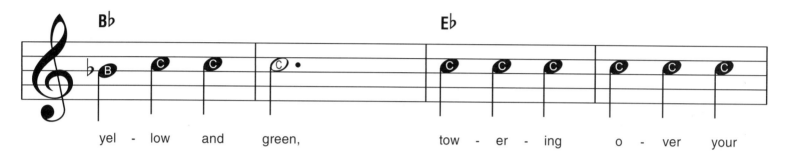

yel - low and green, tow - er - ing o - ver your

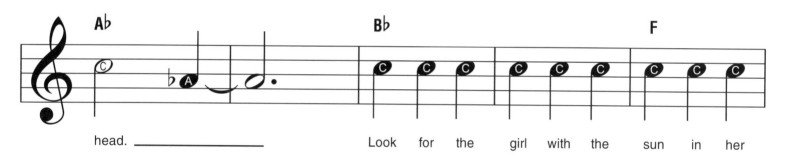

head. _____ Look for the girl with the sun in her

Slower beat

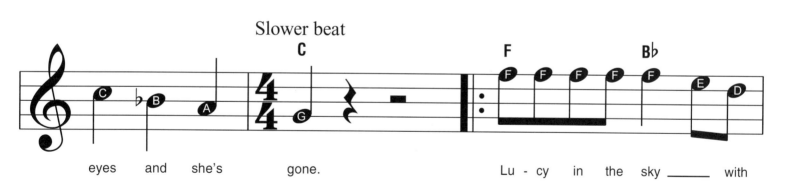

eyes and she's gone. Lu - cy in the sky _____ with

Play 3 times

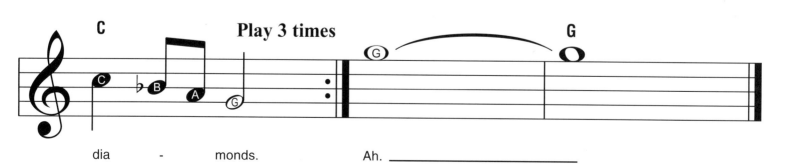

dia - monds. Ah. _____

Magical Mystery Tour

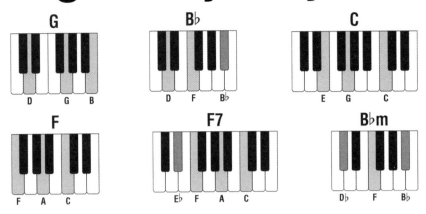

Words and Music by John Lennon
and Paul McCartney

Brightly

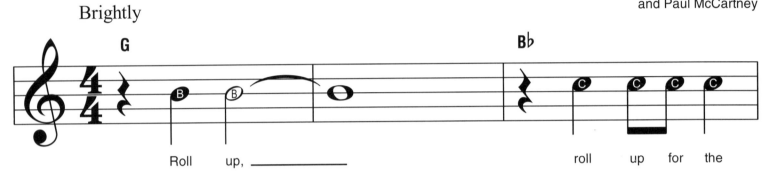

Roll up, _____ roll up for the

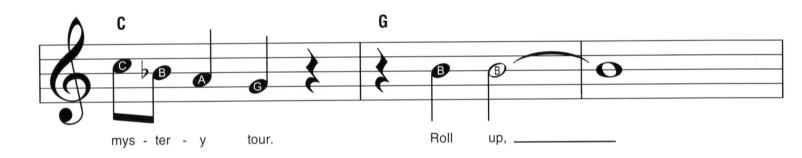

mys - ter - y tour. Roll up, _____

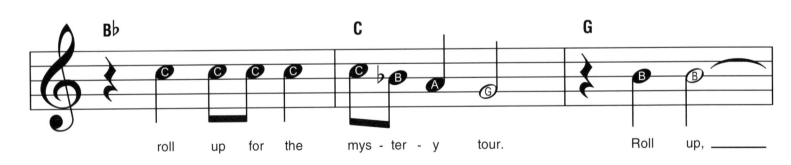

roll up for the mys - ter - y tour. Roll up, _____

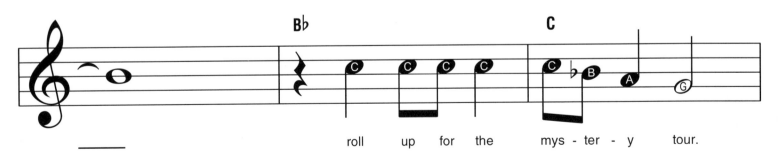

_____ roll up for the mys - ter - y tour.

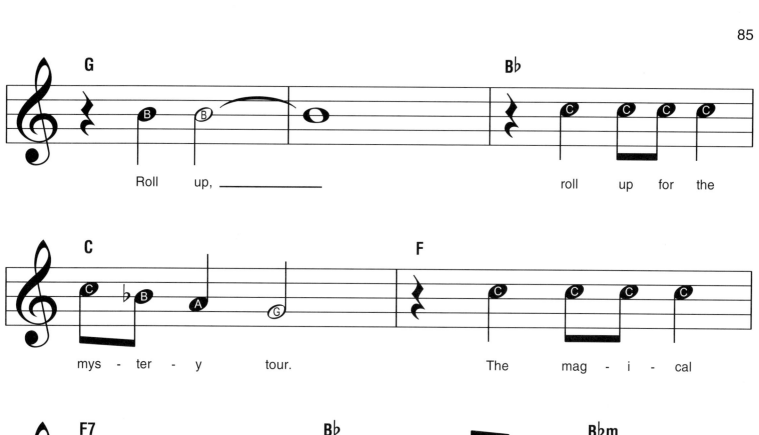

Roll up, _____ roll up for the mys - ter - y tour. The mag - i - cal

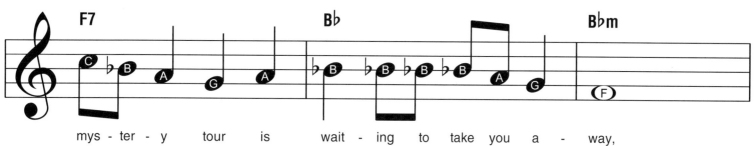

mys - ter - y tour is wait - ing to take you a - way,

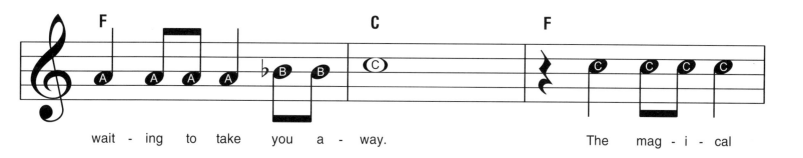

wait - ing to take you a - way. The mag - i - cal

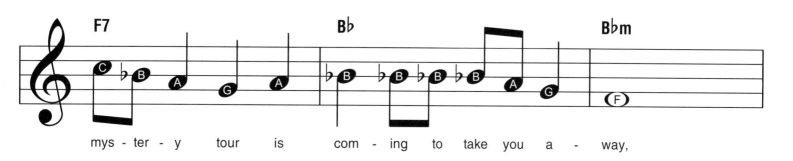

mys - ter - y tour is com - ing to take you a - way,

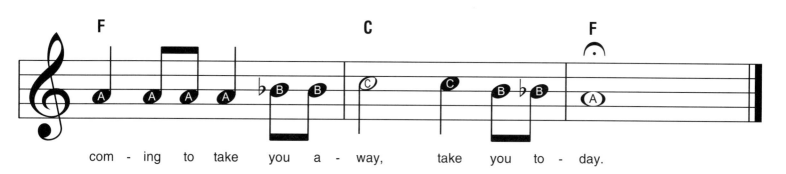

com - ing to take you a - way, take you to - day.

Michelle

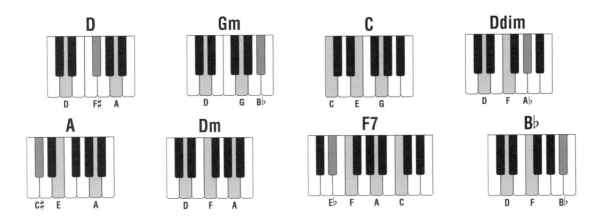

Words and Music by John Lennon
and Paul McCartney

Moderately

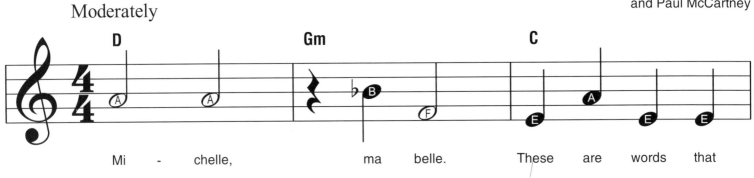

Mi - chelle,　　　　ma belle.　These are words that

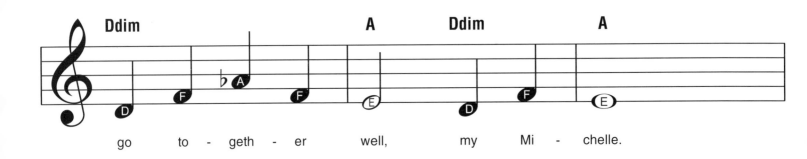

go to - geth - er well, my Mi - chelle.

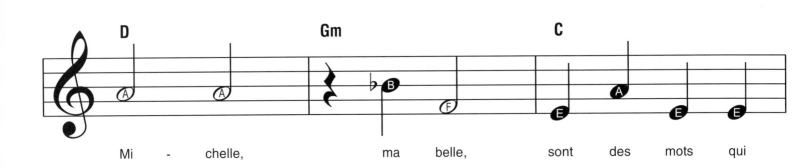

Mi - chelle,　　　　ma belle,　sont des mots qui

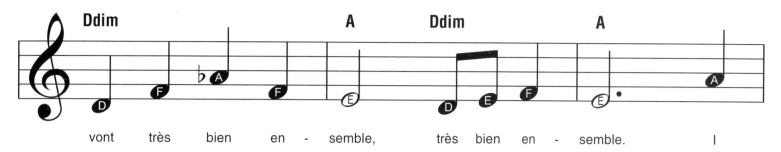

vont très bien en - semble, très bien en - semble. I

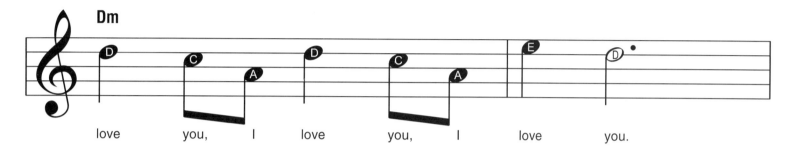

love you, I love you, I love you.

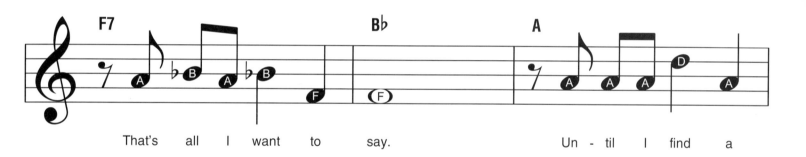

That's all I want to say. Un - til I find a

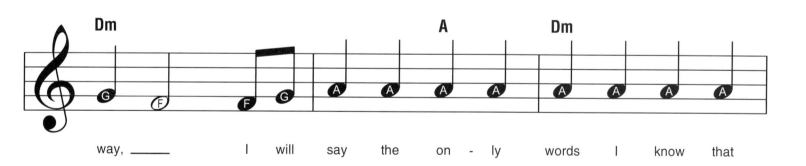

way, _____ I will say the on - ly words I know that

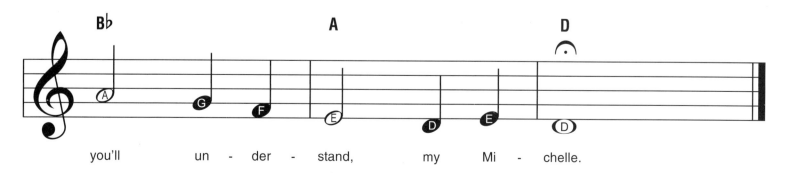

you'll un - der - stand, my Mi - chelle.

Norwegian Wood
(This Bird Has Flown)

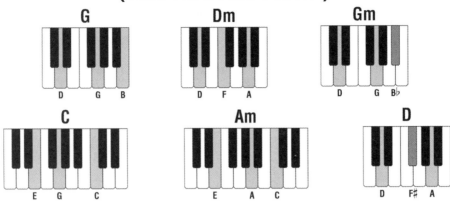

Words and Music by John Lennon
and Paul McCartney

Moderately, with a lilt

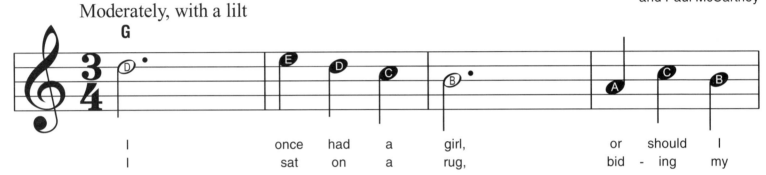

I   once had a girl,   or should I
I   sat on a rug,   bid - ing my

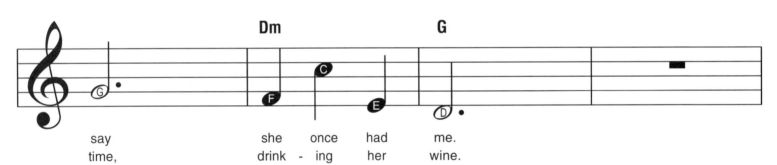

say   she once had me.
time,   drink - ing her wine.

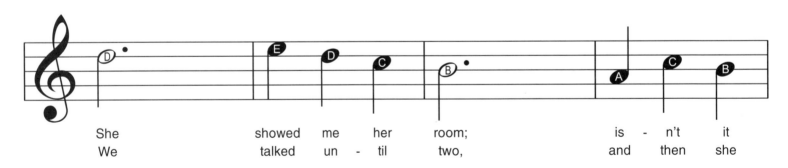

She   showed me her room;   is - n't it
We   talked un - til two,   and then she

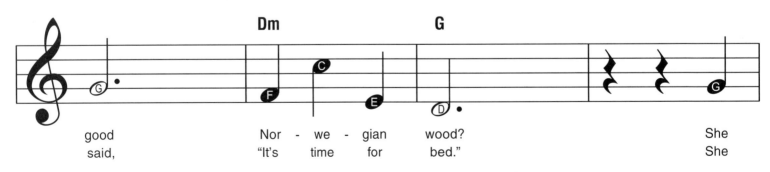

good   Nor - we - gian wood?   She
said,   "It's time for bed."   She

Nowhere Man

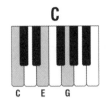 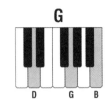 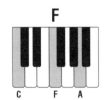 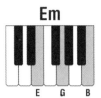

Words and Music by John Lennon
and Paul McCartney

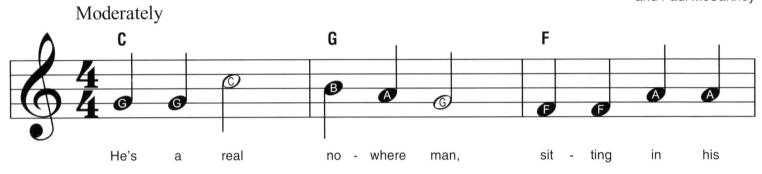

He's a real no - where man, sit - ting in his

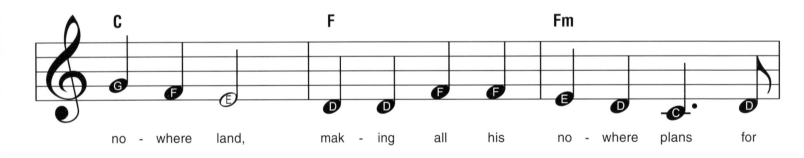

no - where land, mak - ing all his no - where plans for

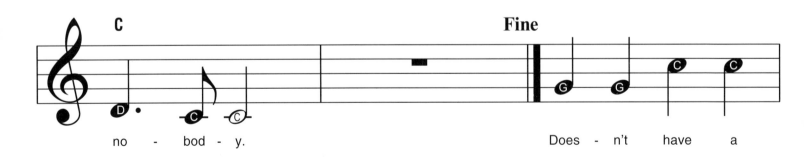

no - bod - y. Does - n't have a

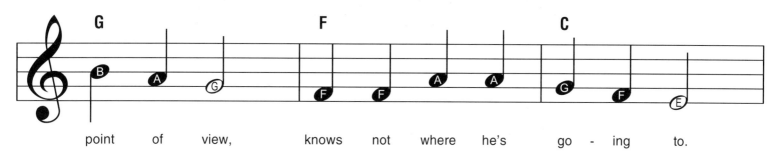

point of view, knows not where he's go - ing to.

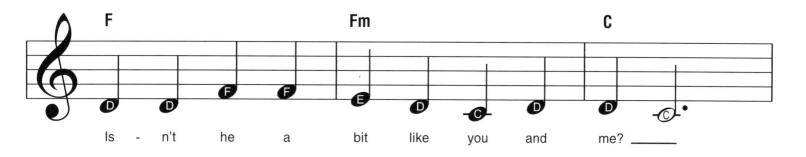

Is - n't he a bit like you and me? _____

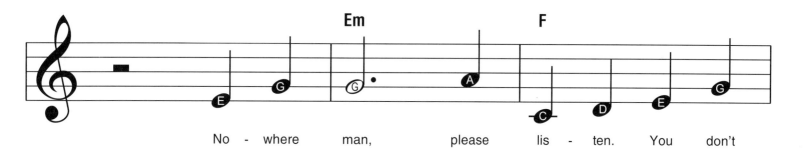

No - where man, please lis - ten. You don't

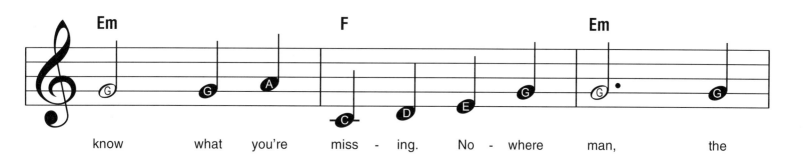

know what you're miss - ing. No - where man, the

D.C. al Fine
(Return to beginning
and play to Fine)

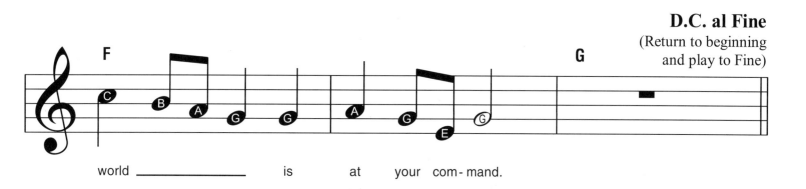

world _____ is at your com - mand.

Ob-La-Di, Ob-La-Da

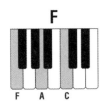 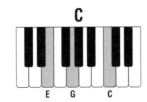 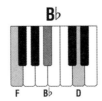 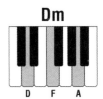 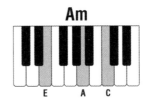

Words and Music by John Lennon
and Paul McCartney

Moderately fast

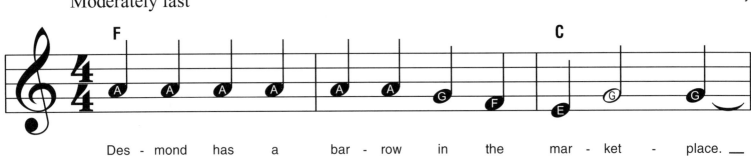

Des - mond has a bar - row in the mar - ket - place. _

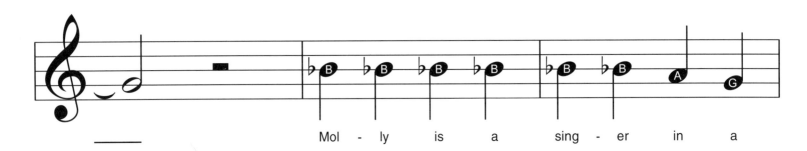

_ Mol - ly is a sing - er in a

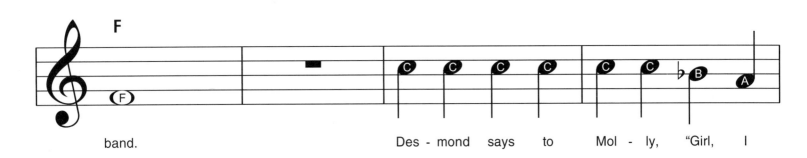

band. Des - mond says to Mol - ly, "Girl, I

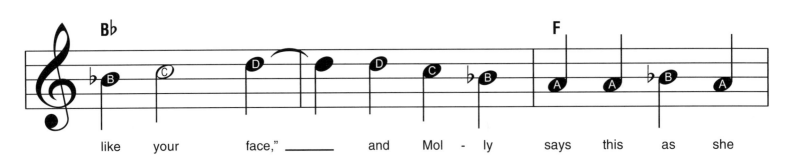

like your face," _____ and Mol - ly says this as she

Octopus's Garden

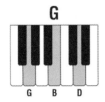
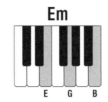
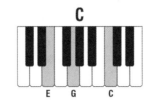
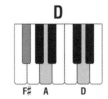

Words and Music by
Richard Starkey

Brightly

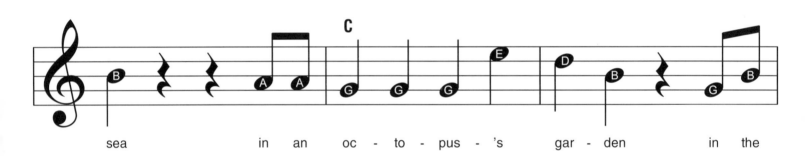

I'd like to be   un - der the

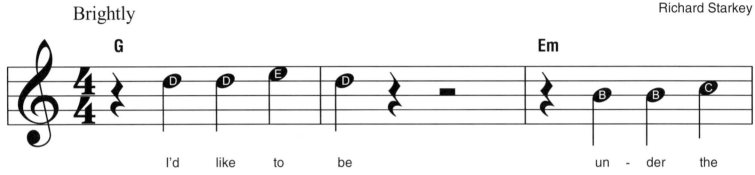

sea   in an oc - to - pus - 's gar - den   in the

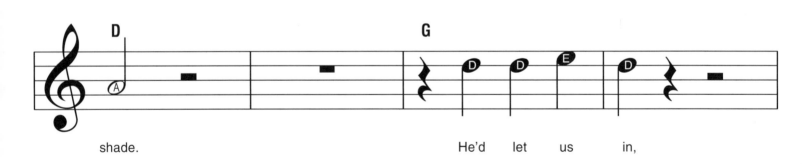

shade.   He'd let us in,

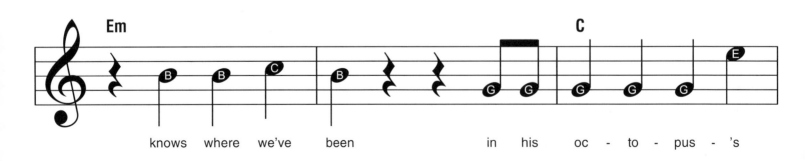

knows where we've been   in his oc - to - pus - 's

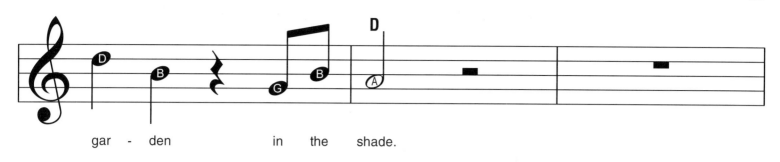

gar - den   in the shade.

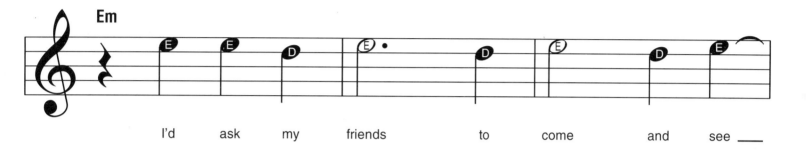

I'd ask my friends   to   come and see ___

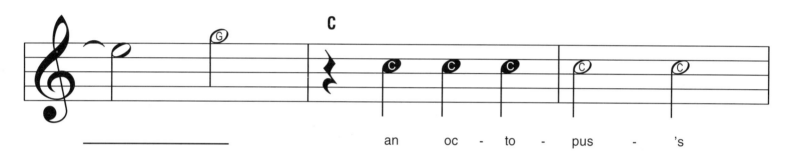

_____   an oc - to - pus - 's

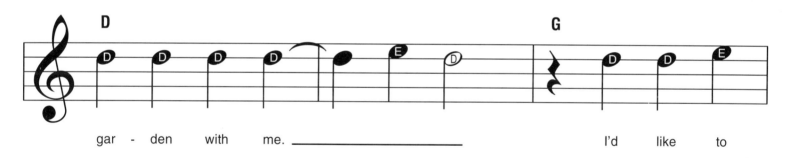

gar - den with me. _____   I'd like to

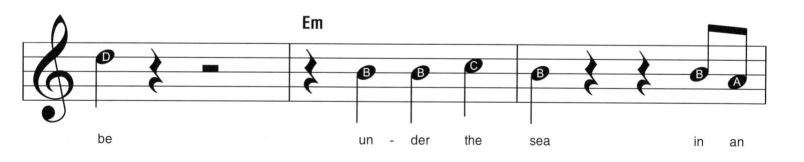

be   un - der the sea   in an

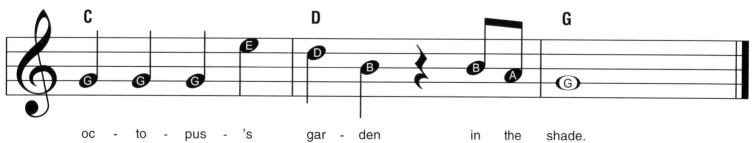

oc - to - pus - 's gar - den   in the shade.

Paperback Writer

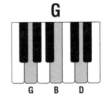
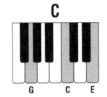

Words and Music by John Lennon
and Paul McCartney

Moderately fast

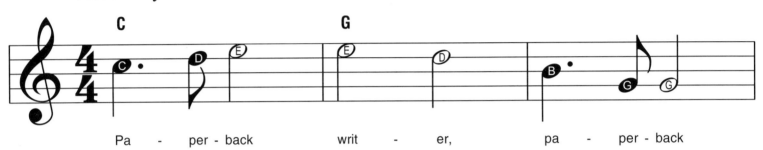

Pa - per - back writ - er, pa - per - back

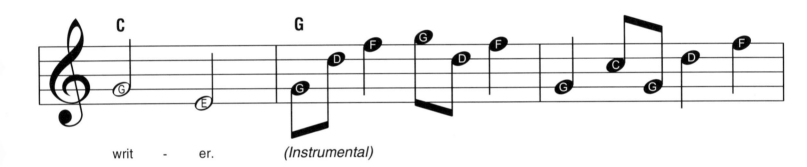

writ - er. (Instrumental)

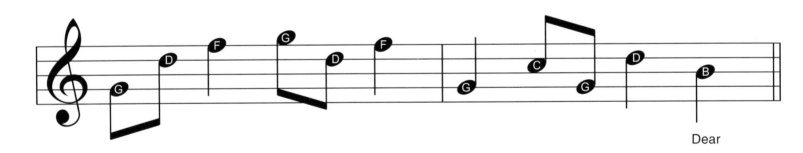

Dear

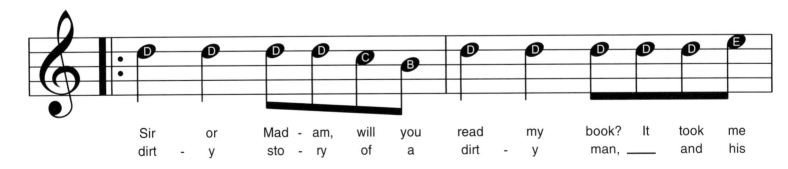

Sir or Mad - am, will you read my book? It took me
dirt - y sto - ry of a dirt - y man, _____ and his

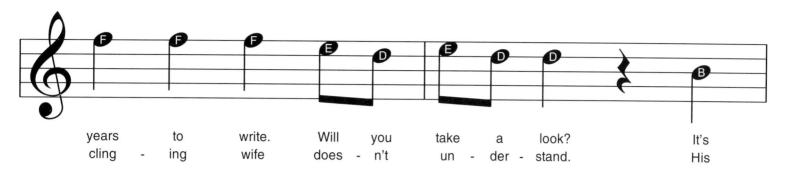

years   to   write.   Will   you   take   a   look?   It's
cling - ing   wife   does - n't   un - der - stand.   His

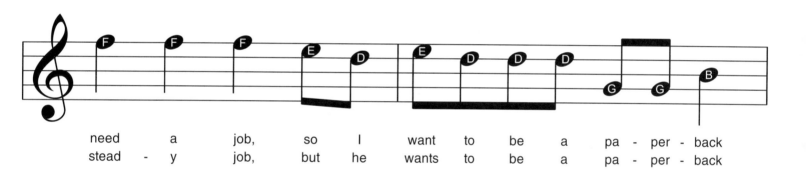

based   on   a   nov - el   by   a   man   named   Lear,   and   I
son   is _____ work - ing   for   the   Dai - ly   Mail.   It's   a

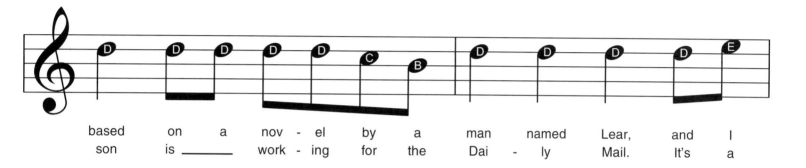

need   a   job,   so   I   want   to   be   a   pa - per - back
stead - y   job,   but   he   wants   to   be   a   pa - per - back

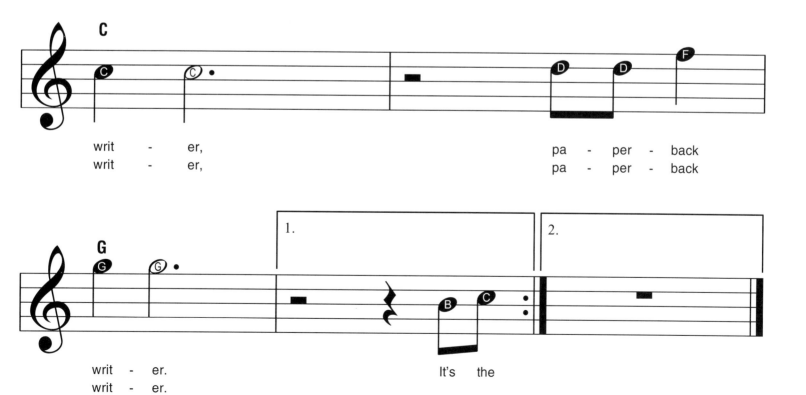

writ - er,   pa - per - back
writ - er,   pa - per - back

writ - er.   It's   the
writ - er.

Penny Lane

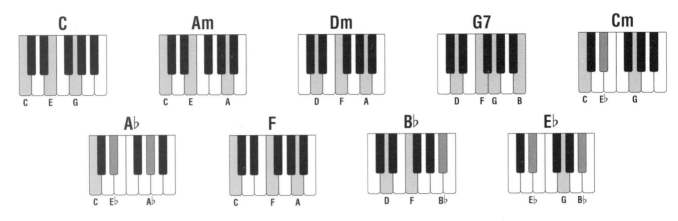

Words and Music by John Lennon
and Paul McCartney

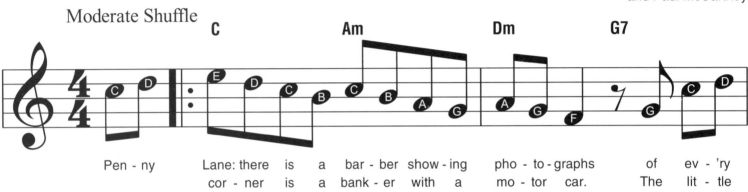

Moderate Shuffle

Pen - ny Lane: there is a bar - ber show - ing a pho - to - graphs of ev - 'ry
cor - ner is a bank - er with a mo - tor car. The lit - tle

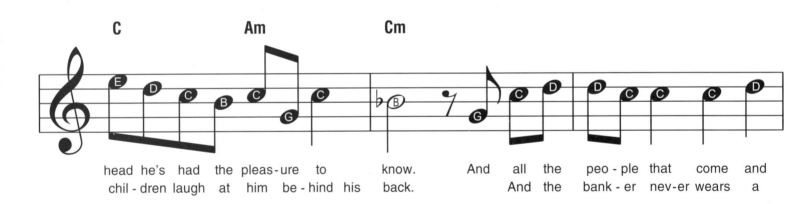

head he's had the pleas - ure to know. And all the peo - ple that come and
chil - dren laugh at him be - hind his back. And the bank - er nev - er wears a

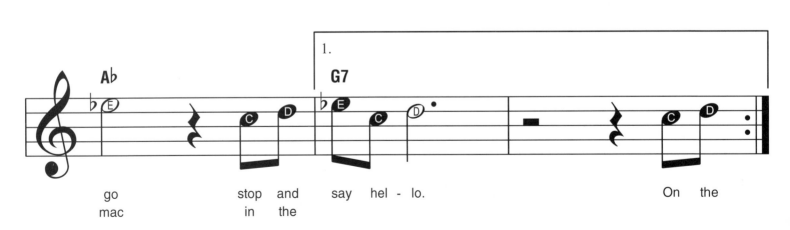

go stop and say hel - lo. On the
mac in the

Revolution

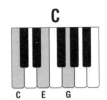
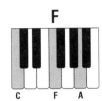
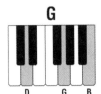
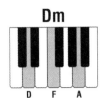
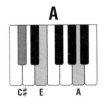

Words and Music by John Lennon
and Paul McCartney

Rock Shuffle

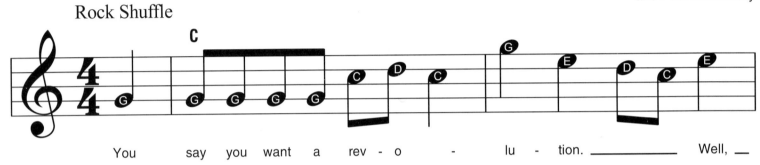

You say you want a rev - o - lu - tion. _____ Well, __

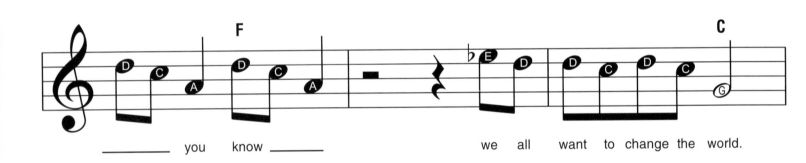

_____ you know _____ we all want to change the world.

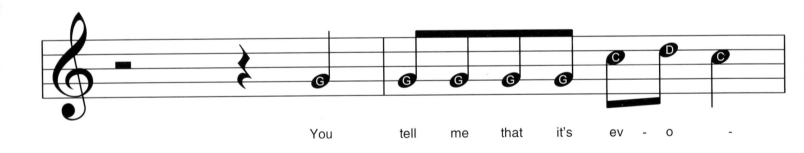

You tell me that it's ev - o -

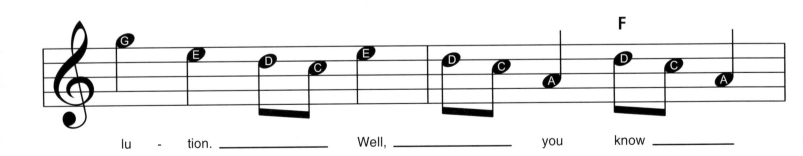

lu - tion. _____ Well, _____ you know _____

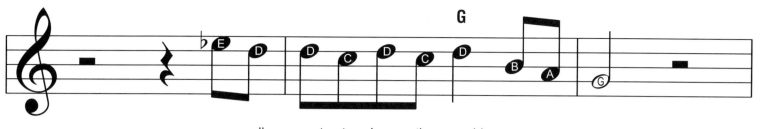

we all want to change the world. _____

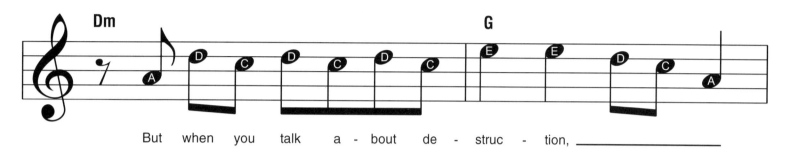

But when you talk a - bout de - struc - tion, _____

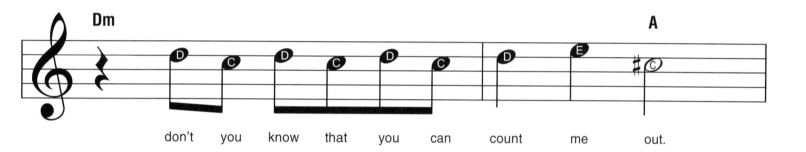

don't you know that you can count me out.

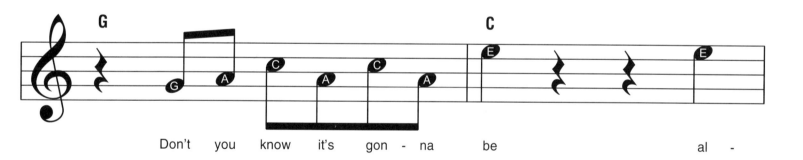

Don't you know it's gon - na be al -

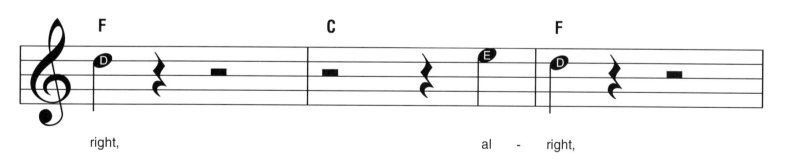

right, al - right,

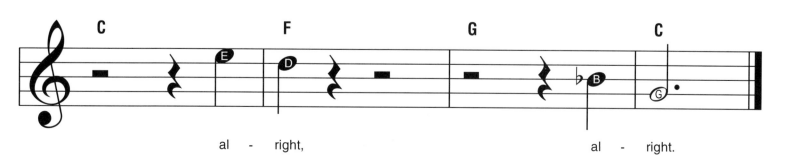

al - right, al - right.

She Loves You

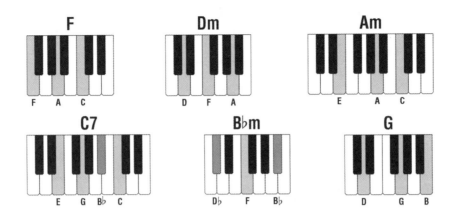

Words and Music by John Lennon
and Paul McCartney

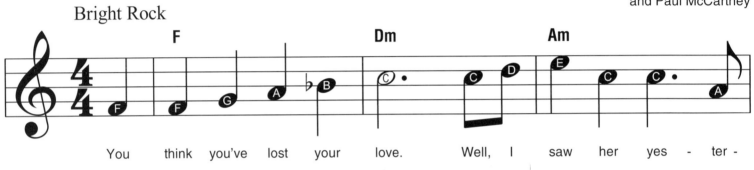

You think you've lost your love. Well, I saw her yes - ter -

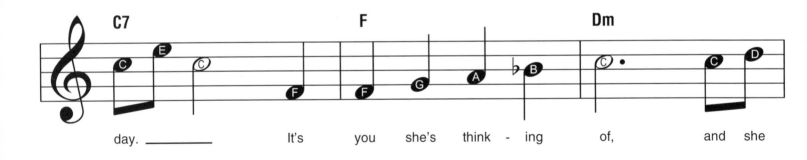

day. _____ It's you she's think - ing of, and she

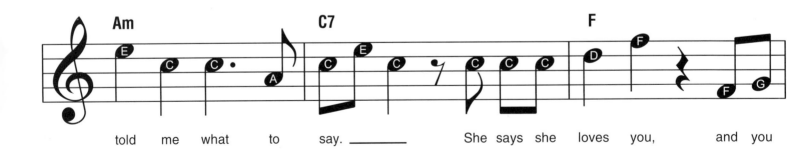

told me what to say. _____ She says she loves you, and you

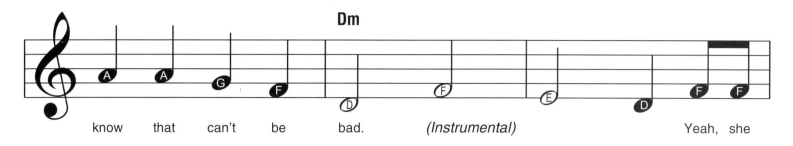

know that can't be bad. *(Instrumental)* Yeah, she

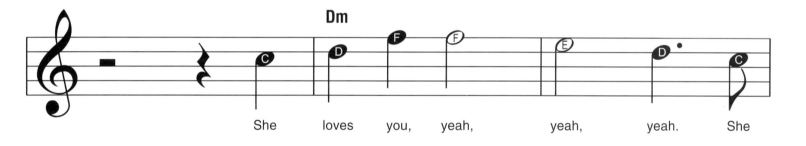

loves you and you know you should be glad.

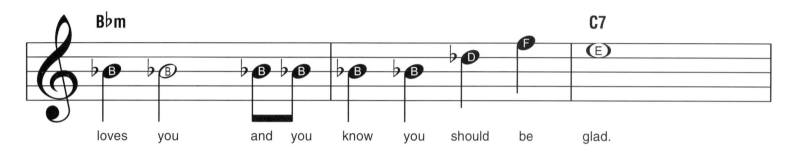

She loves you, yeah, yeah, yeah. She

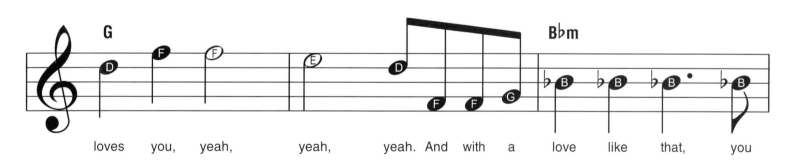

loves you, yeah, yeah, yeah. And with a love like that, you

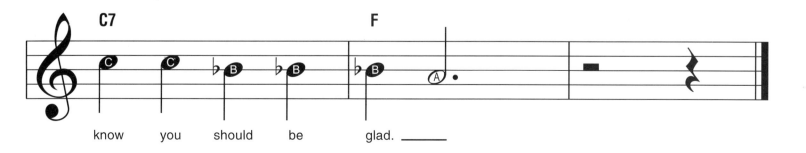

know you should be glad. _____

Something

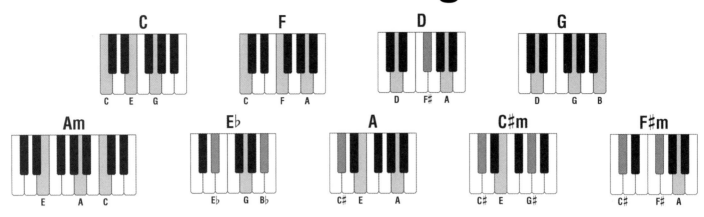

Words and Music by
George Harrison

Moderately slow

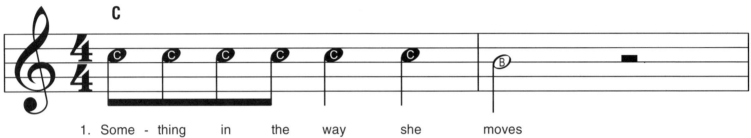

1. Some - thing   in   the   way   she   moves
2., 3. *See additional lyrics*

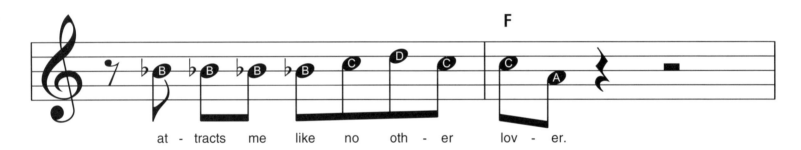

at - tracts   me   like   no   oth - er   lov - er.

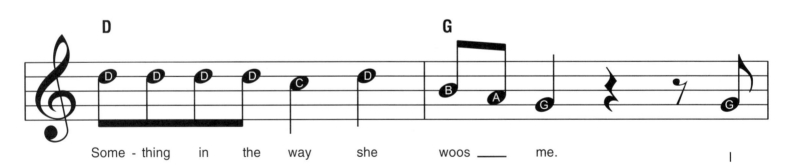

Some - thing   in   the   way   she   woos ____ me.

To Coda ⊕

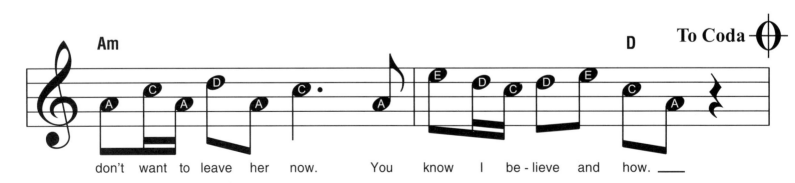

don't   want   to   leave   her   now.   You   know   I   be - lieve   and   how. ____

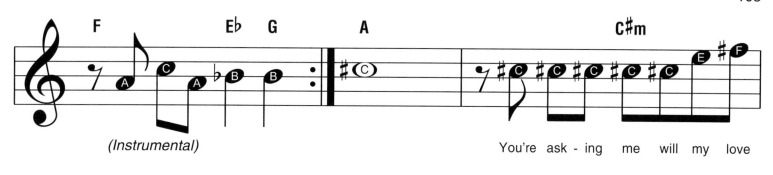

(Instrumental)

You're ask - ing me will my love

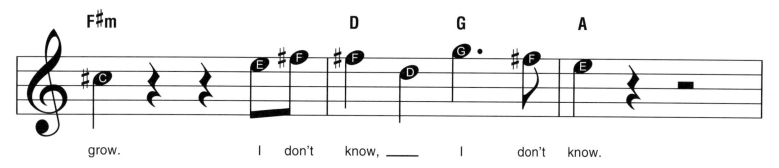

grow. I don't know, _____ I don't know.

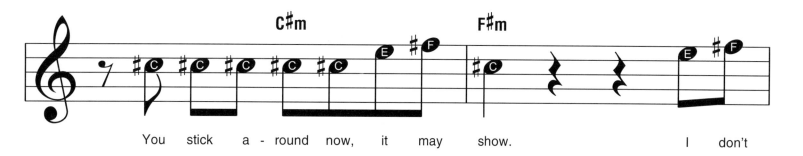

You stick a - round now, it may show. I don't

D.C. al Coda
(Return to beginning,
play to ⊕ and skip to Coda)

CODA

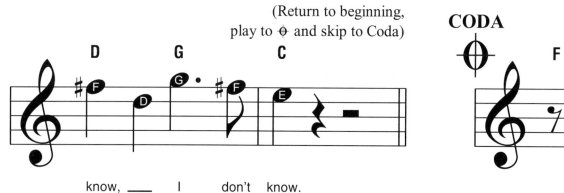

know, _____ I don't know.

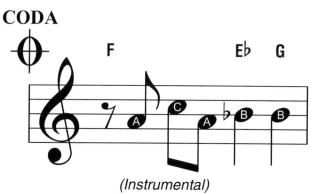

(Instrumental)

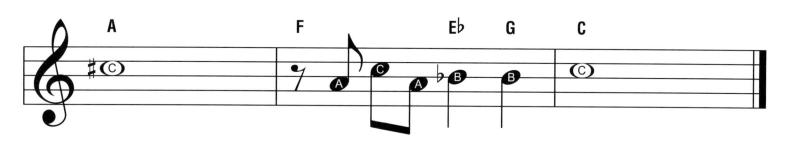

Additional Lyrics

2. Somewhere in her smile she knows
That I don't need no other lover.
Something in her style that shows me.
I don't want to leave her now.
You know I believe and how.

3. Something in the way she knows,
And all I have to do is think of her.
Something in the things she shows me.
I don't want to leave her now.
You know I believe and how.

Strawberry Fields Forever

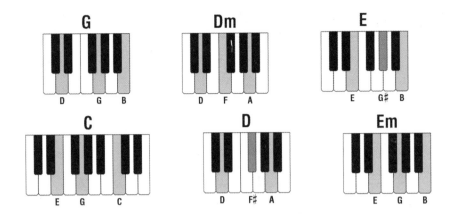

Words and Music by John Lennon
and Paul McCartney

Moderately slow

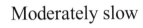

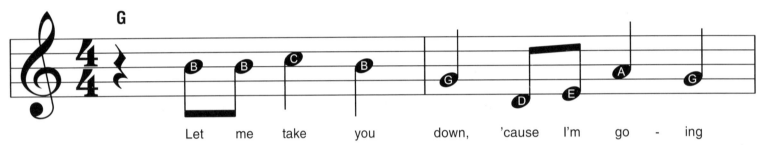

Let me take you down, 'cause I'm go - ing

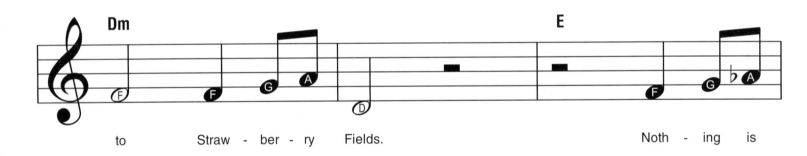

to Straw - ber - ry Fields. Noth - ing is

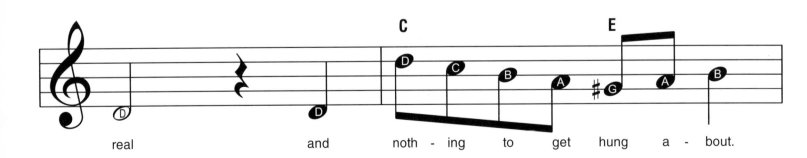

real and noth - ing to get hung a - bout.

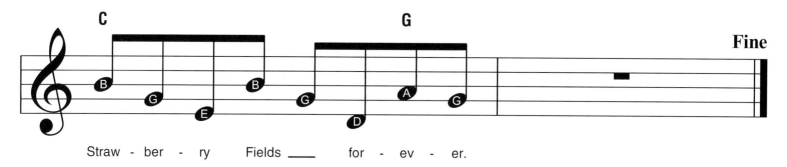

Straw - ber - ry Fields ___ for - ev - er. **Fine**

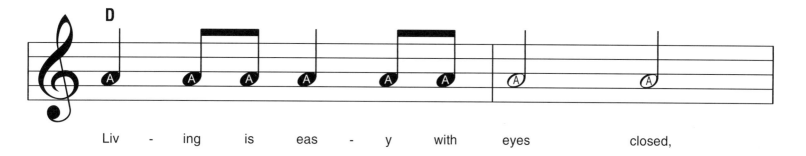

Liv - ing is eas - y with eyes closed,

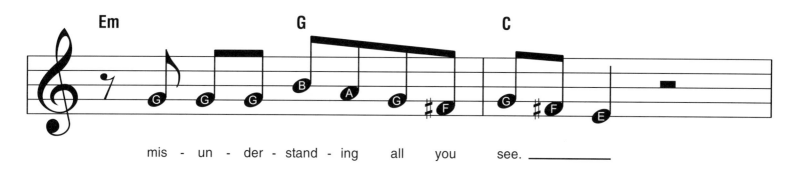

mis - un - der - stand - ing all you see. _____

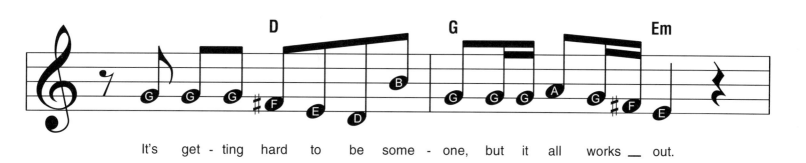

It's get - ting hard to be some - one, but it all works __ out.

D.C. al Fine
(Return to beginning
and play to Fine)

It does - n't mat - ter much to me.

Ticket to Ride

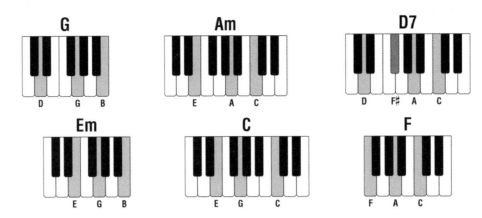

Words and Music by John Lennon
and Paul McCartney

Moderately

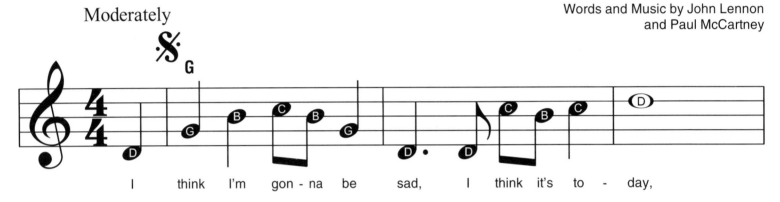

I think I'm gon - na be sad, I think it's to - day,

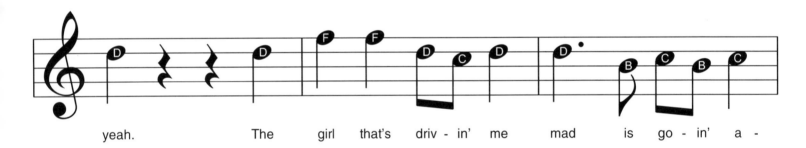

yeah. The girl that's driv - in' me mad is go - in' a -

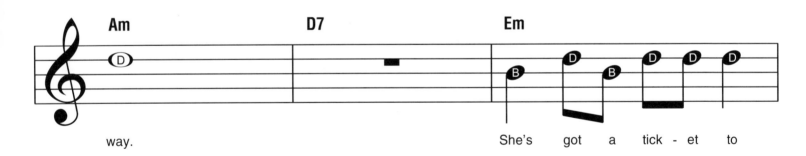

way. She's got a tick - et to

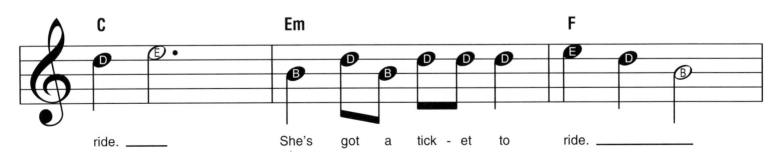

ride. _____ She's got a tick - et to ride. _____

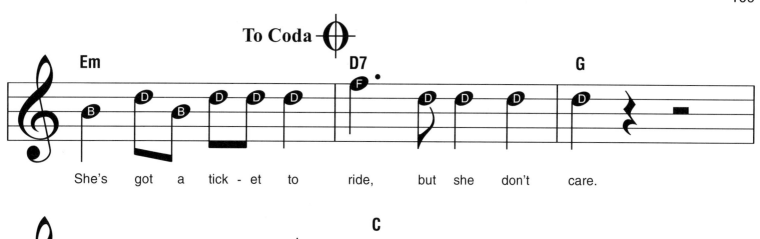

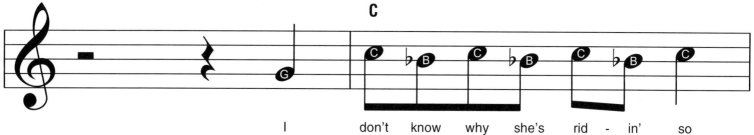

She's got a tick - et to ride, but she don't care.

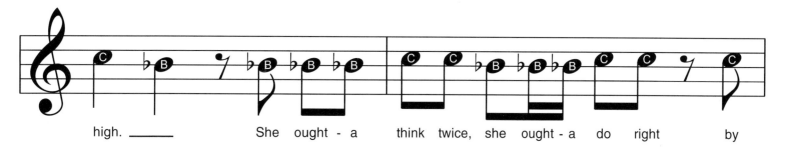

I don't know why she's rid - in' so

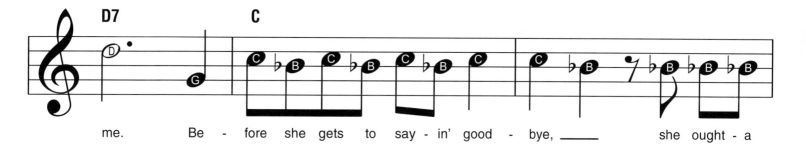

high. _____ She ought - a think twice, she ought - a do right by

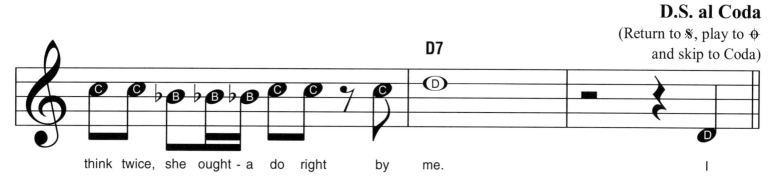

me. Be - fore she gets to say - in' good - bye, _____ she ought - a

D.S. al Coda
(Return to 𝄋, play to ⊕
and skip to Coda)

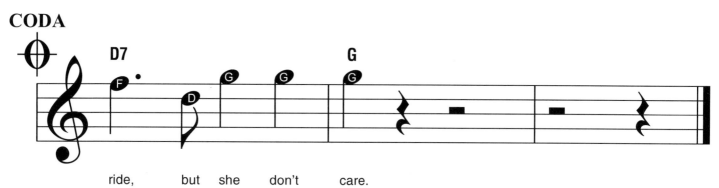

think twice, she ought - a do right by me. I

CODA

ride, but she don't care.

Twist and Shout

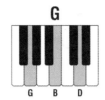
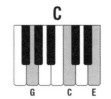
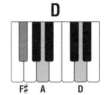

Words and Music by Bert Russell
and Phil Medley

Moderately fast
(no chord)

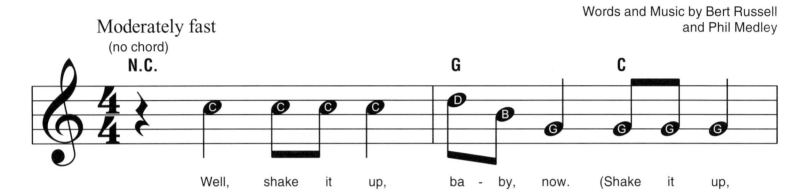

Well, shake it up, ba - by, now. (Shake it up,

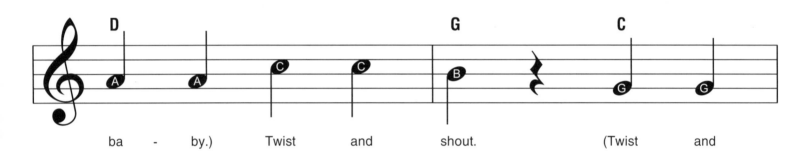

ba - by.) Twist and shout. (Twist and

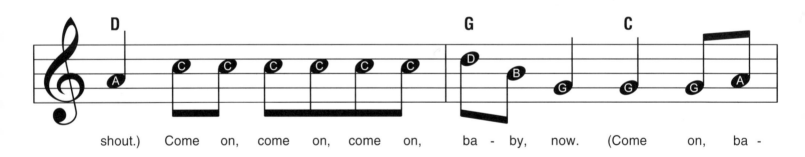

shout.) Come on, come on, come on, ba - by, now. (Come on, ba-

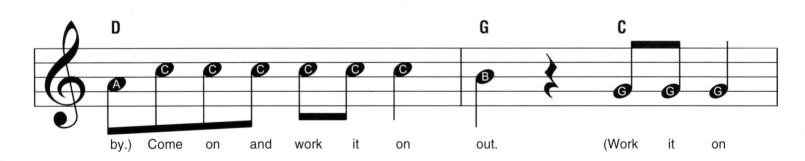

by.) Come on and work it on out. (Work it on

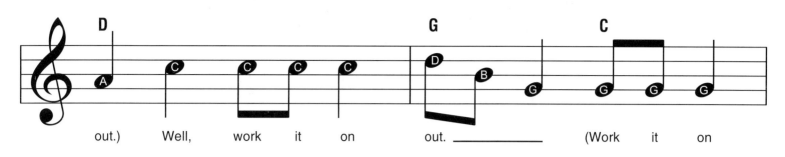

out.) Well, work it on out. _____ (Work it on

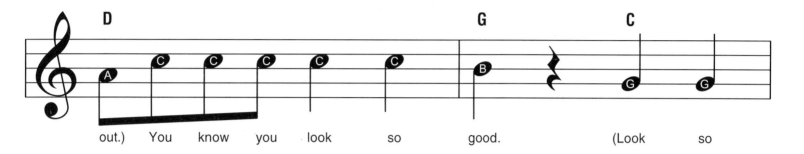

out.) You know you look so good. (Look so

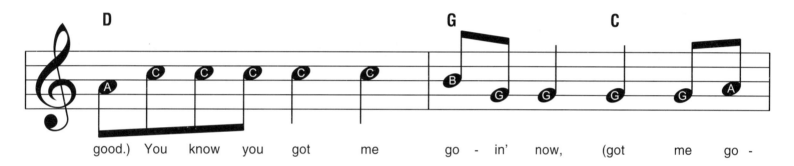

good.) You know you got me go - in' now, (got me go -

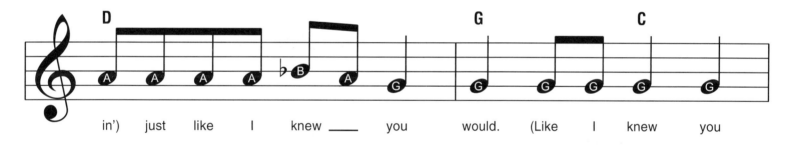

in') just like I knew ____ you would. (Like I knew you

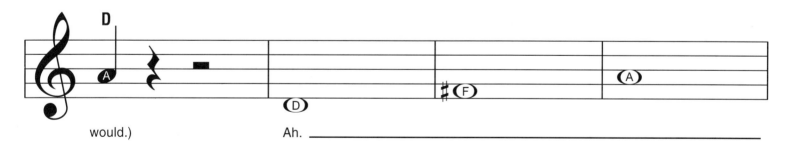

would.) Ah. _____

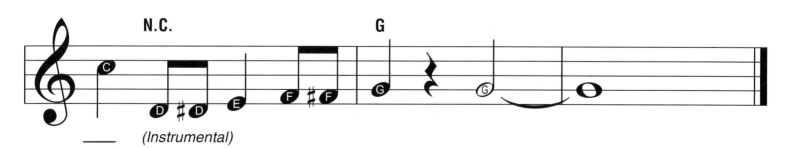

____ (Instrumental)

We Can Work It Out

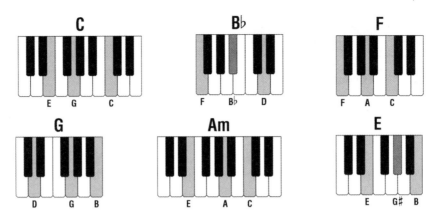

Words and Music by John Lennon
and Paul McCartney

Moderately

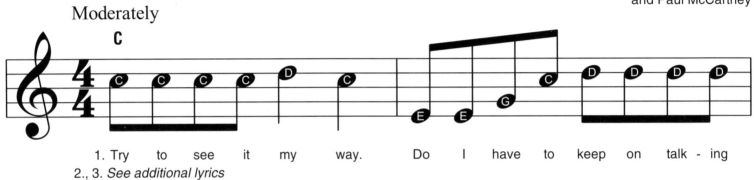

1. Try to see it my way. Do I have to keep on talk-ing
2., 3. *See additional lyrics*

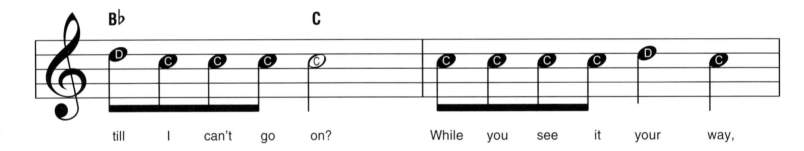

till I can't go on? While you see it your way,

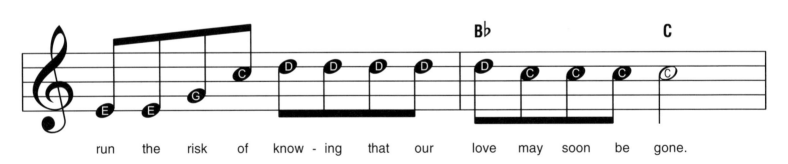

run the risk of know-ing that our love may soon be gone.

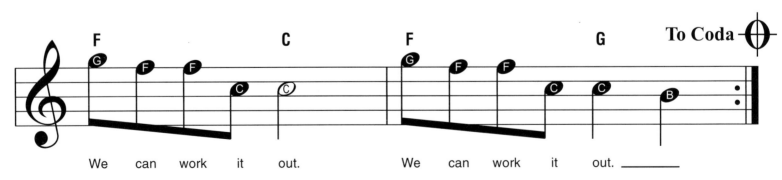

We can work it out. We can work it out. _____

Life is ver - y short and there's no time

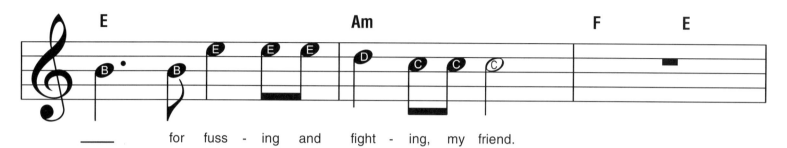

_____ for fuss - ing and fight - ing, my friend.

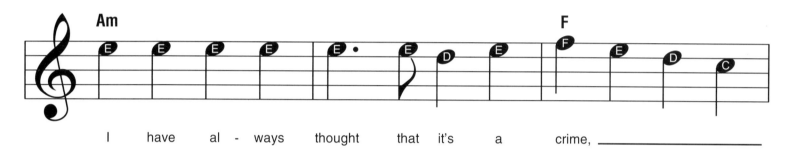

I have al - ways thought that it's a crime, _____

D.C. al Coda
(Return to beginning,
play to ⊕ and skip to Coda)

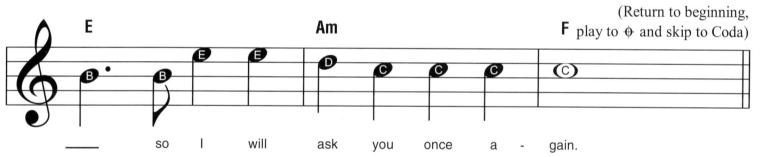

_____ so I will ask you once a - gain.

CODA

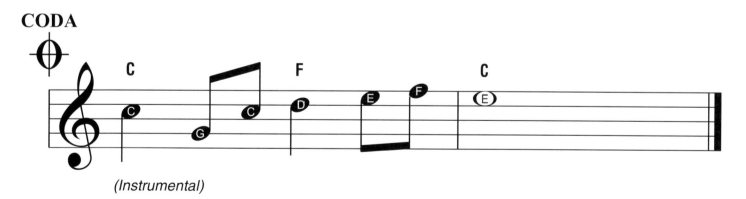

(Instrumental)

Additional Lyrics

2. Think of what you're saying.
   You can get it wrong and still you think that it's alright.
   Think of what I'm saying.
   We can work it out and get it straight or say goodnight.
   We can work it out. We can work it out.

3. Try to see it my way.
   Only time will tell if I am right or I am wrong.
   While you see it your way,
   There's a chance that we might fall apart before too long.
   We can work it out. We can work it out.

When I'm Sixty-Four

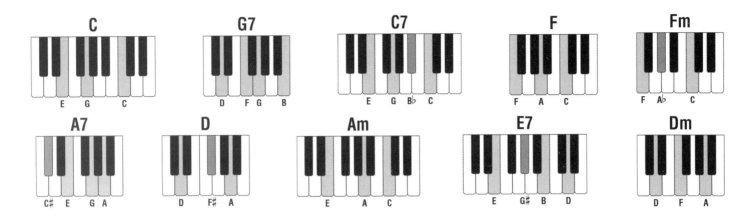

Words and Music by John Lennon
and Paul McCartney

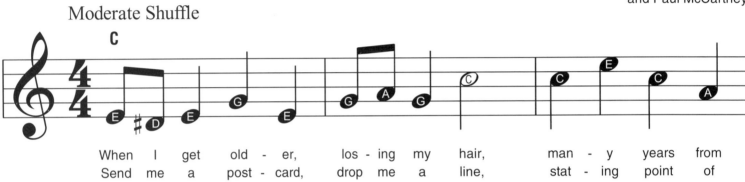

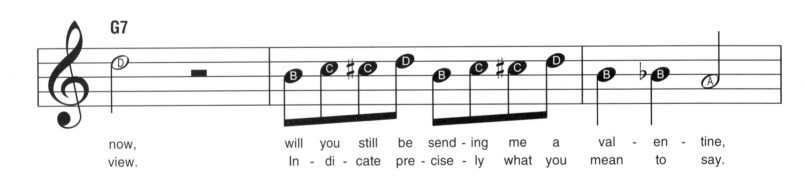

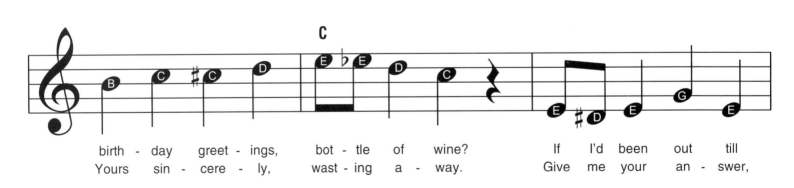

quar - ter to three, would you lock the door?
fill in a form, mine for - ev - er - more.

Will you still need me?

Will you still feed me when I'm six - ty - four?

Ooh. _____

You'll be old - er, too.

Ah, _____ and if you say the word, _____

I could stay with you.

D.C. al Fine
(Return to beginning
and play to Fine)

Fine

While My Guitar Gently Weeps

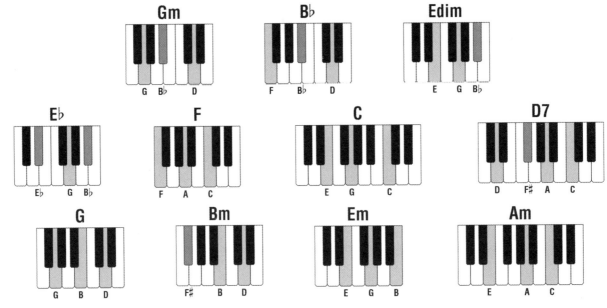

Words and Music by
George Harrison

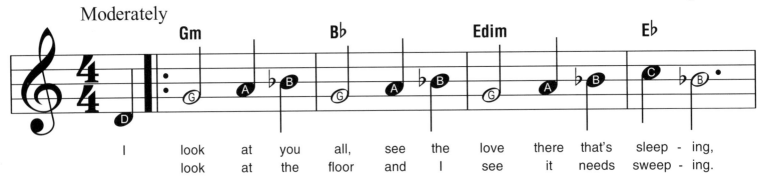

I look at you all, see the love there that's sleep-ing,
look at the all, floor see and I love see it needs sweep-ing.

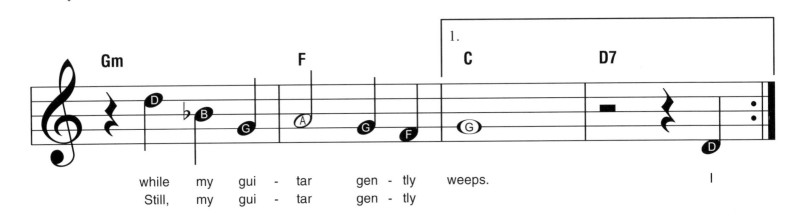

while my gui-tar gen-tly weeps.
Still, my gui-tar gen-tly

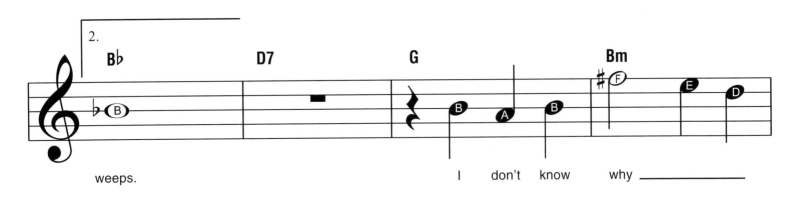

weeps.   I don't know why _____

With a Little Help from My Friends

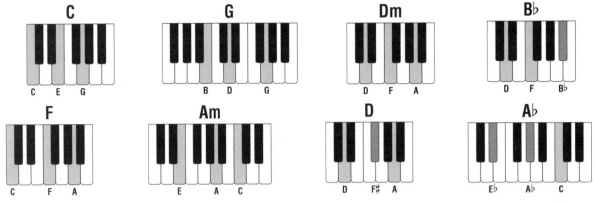

Words and Music by John Lennon
and Paul McCartney

Moderate Shuffle

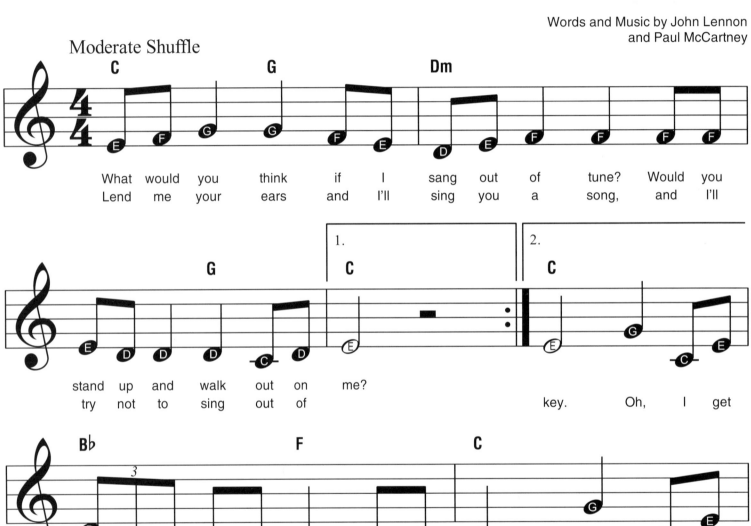

What would you think if I sang out of tune? Would you
Lend me your ears and I'll sing you a song, and I'll

stand up and walk out on me?
try not to sing out of key. Oh, I get

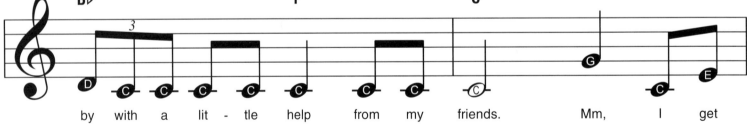

by with a lit- tle help from my friends. Mm, I get

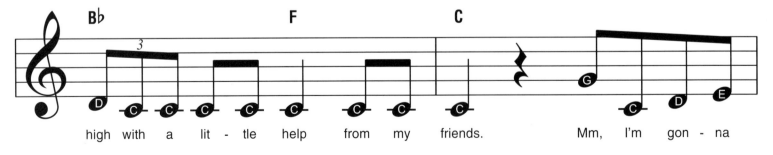

high with a lit- tle help from my friends. Mm, I'm gon- na

Yellow Submarine

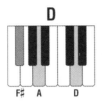
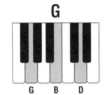
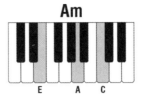

Words and Music by John Lennon
and Paul McCartney

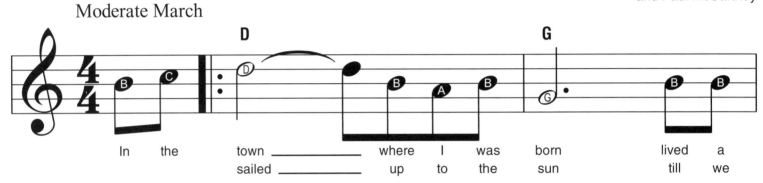

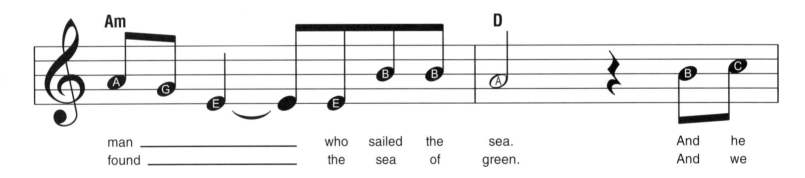

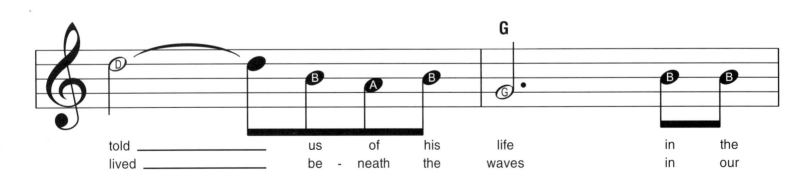

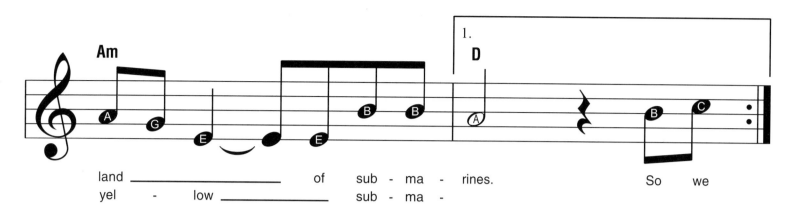

land _____ of sub - ma - rines. So we
yel - low _____ sub - ma -

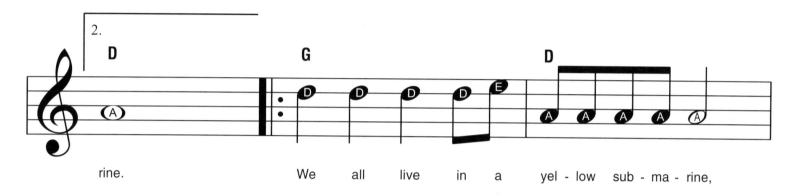

rine. We all live in a yel - low sub - ma - rine,

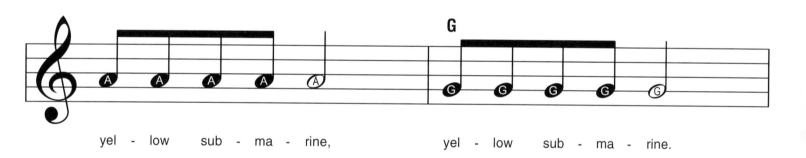

yel - low sub - ma - rine, yel - low sub - ma - rine.

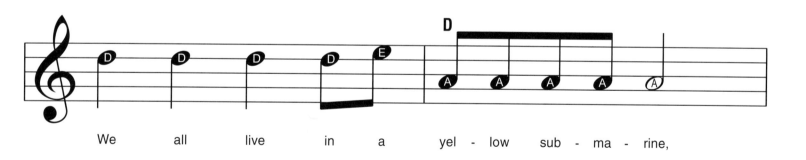

We all live in a yel - low sub - ma - rine,

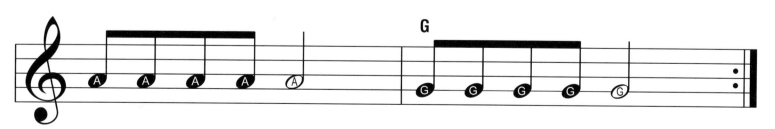

yel - low sub - ma - rine, yel - low sub - ma - rine.

Yesterday

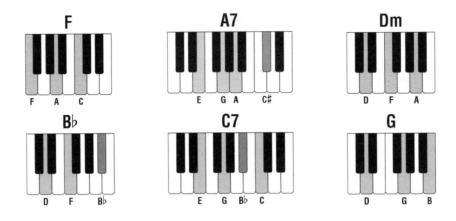

Words and Music by John Lennon
and Paul McCartney

Moderately slow

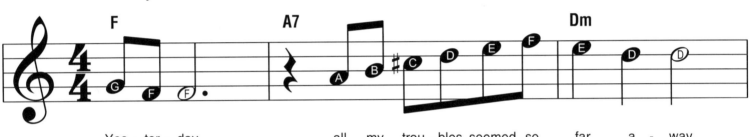

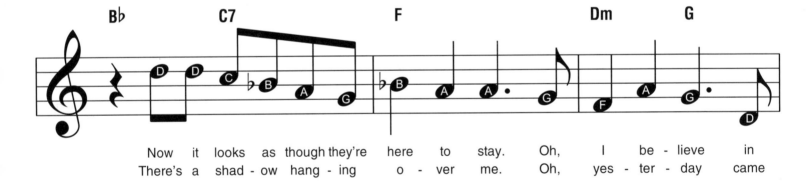

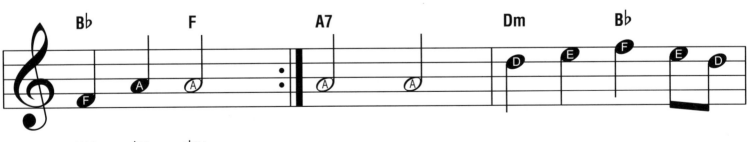

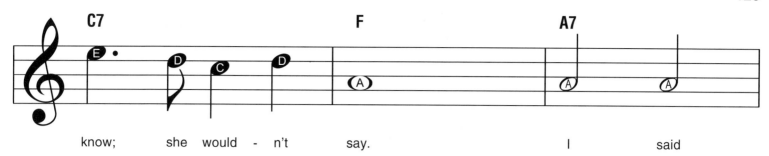

know; she would - n't say. I said

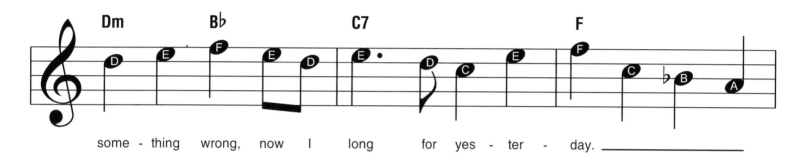

some - thing wrong, now I long for yes - ter - day. _____

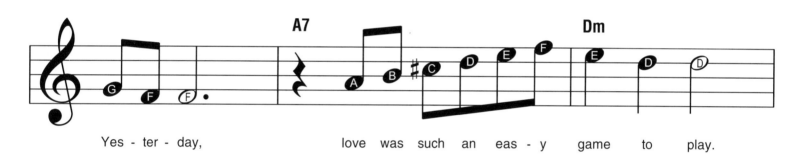

Yes - ter - day, love was such an eas - y game to play.

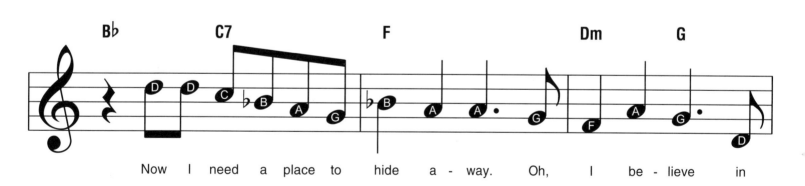

Now I need a place to hide a - way. Oh, I be - lieve in

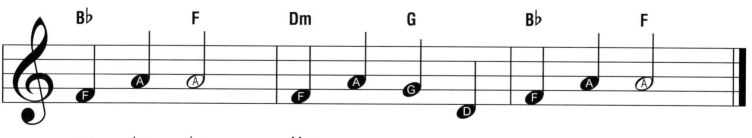

yes - ter - day. Mm. _____

You've Got to Hide Your Love Away

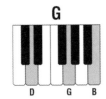
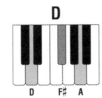
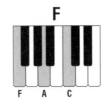
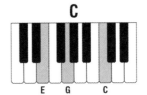

Words and Music by John Lennon
and Paul McCartney

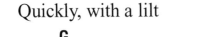
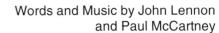

Quickly, with a lilt

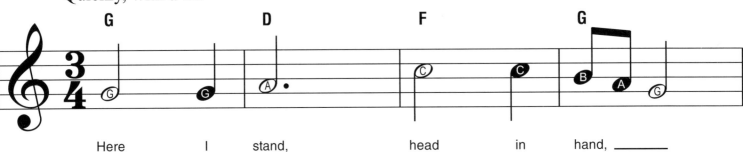

Here   I   stand,   head   in   hand, _____
Ev - 'ry - where   peo - ple   stare _____

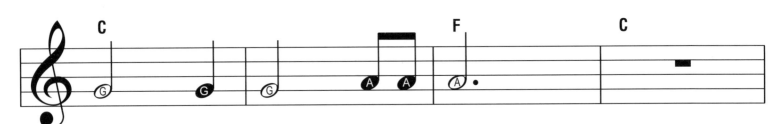

turn   my   face   to   the   wall.
each   and _____   ev - 'ry   day.

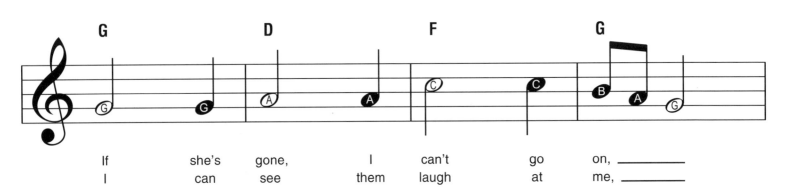

If   she's   gone,   I   can't   go   on, _____
I   can   see   them   laugh   at   me, _____

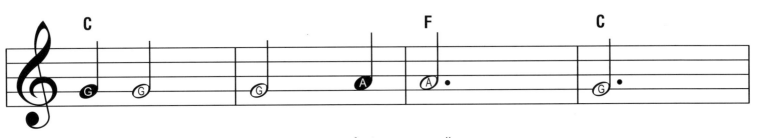

feel - ing   two   foot   small. _____
and   I   hear   them   say: _____

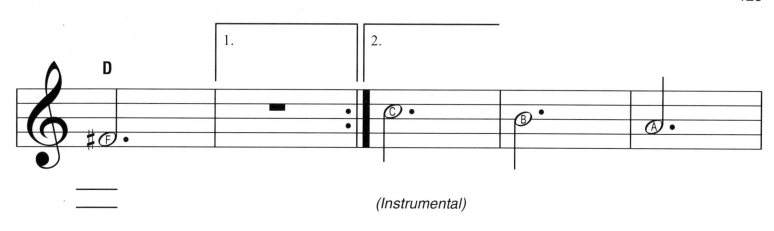

(Instrumental)

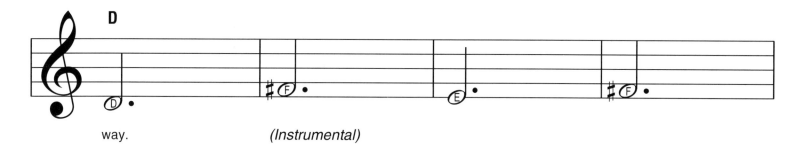

Hey, _____ you've got to hide your _____ love a -

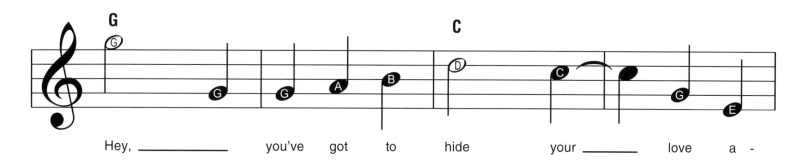

way.   (Instrumental)

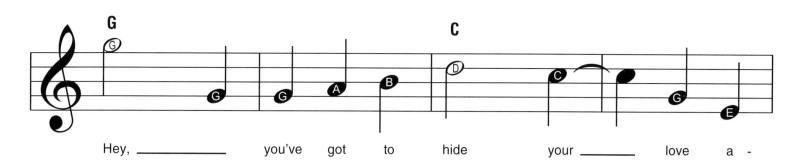

Hey, _____ you've got to hide your _____ love a -

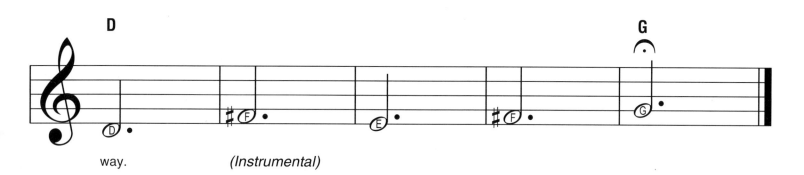

way.   (Instrumental)

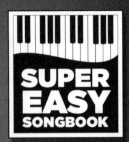

HAL LEONARD PRESENTS
FAKE BOOKS FOR BEGINNERS!

Entry-level fake books! These books feature larger-than-most fake book notation with simplified harmonies and melodies – and all songs are in the key of C. An introduction addresses basic instruction on playing from a fake book.

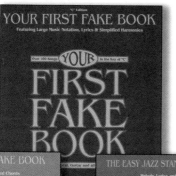

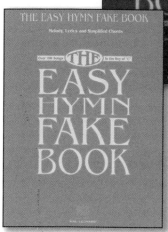

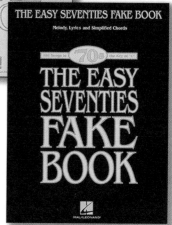

Your First Fake Book
00299529...$22.99

The Easy Fake Book
00240144...$19.99

The Simplified Fake Book
00299494...$22.99

The Beatles Easy Fake Book
00171200 ....$25.00

The Easy Broadway Fake Book
00276670...$19.99

The Easy Children's Fake Book
00240428 ....$19.99

The Easy Christian Fake Book
00240328...$19.99

The Easy Christmas Carols Fake Book
00238187 ....$19.99

The Easy Christmas Songs Fake Book
00277913...$19.99

The Easy Classic Rock Fake Book
00240389 ....$24.99

The Easy Classical Fake Book
00240262...$19.99

The Easy Country Fake Book
00240319...$22.99

The Easy Disney Fake Book
00275405...$24.99

The Easy Folksong Fake Book
00240360...$22.99

The Easy 4-Chord Fake Book
00118752 ....$19.99

The Easy G Major Fake Book
00142279 ....$19.99

The Easy Gospel Fake Book
00240169...$19.99

The Easy Hymn Fake Book
00240207...$19.99

The Easy Jazz Standards Fake Book
00102346...$19.99

The Easy Love Songs Fake Book
00159775 ....$24.99

The Easy Pop/Rock Fake Book
00141667 ....$24.99

The Easy 3-Chord Fake Book
00240388...$19.99

The Easy Worship Fake Book
00240265...$22.99

More of the Easy Worship Fake Book
00240362...$22.99

The Easy '20s Fake Book
00240336 ....$19.99

The Easy '30s Fake Book
00240335 ....$19.99

The Easy '40s Fake Book
00240252...$19.99

The Easy '50s Fake Book
00240255...$22.99

The Easy '60s Fake Book
00240253...$22.99

The Easy '70s Fake Book
00240256...$22.99

The Easy '80s Fake Book
00240340 ....$24.99

The Easy '90s Fake Book
00240341 ....$19.99

HAL•LEONARD®
halleonard.com

*Prices, contents and availability
subject to change without notice.*
0421
128

FOR ORGANS, PIANOS & ELECTRONIC KEYBOARDS

E-Z PLAY® TODAY PUBLICATIONS

The E-Z Play® Today songbook series is the shortest distance between beginning music and playing fun!
*Check out this list of highlights and visit **balleonard.com** for a complete listing of all volumes and songlists.*

HAL•LEONARD®

Prices, contents and availability
subject to change without notice

0421

330